"LIVE SO THAT YOU MAY DESIRE TO LIVE THE SAME LIFE AGAIN AND NOT ONLY ONCE, BUT AN INFINITE NUMBER OF TIMES!" — FRIEDRICH NIETZSCHE ON ETERNAL RECURRENCE

"GREAT. THAT MEANS I'LL HAVE TO SIT THROUGH THE ICE CAPADES AGAIN." — WOODY ALLEN

"THIS IS LIKE THE INTRO TO PHILOSOPHY CLASS THAT YOU WANTED TO TAKE IN COLLEGE BUT COULDN'T BECAUSE IT WASN'T OFFERED." — FORT WORTH STAR-TELEGRAM

ETERNITY IS RIGHT NOW. BUY THIS BOOK TODAY!

PENGUIN BOOKS

HEIDEGGER AND A HIPPO WALK THROUGH THOSE PEARLY GATES

Thomas Cathcart and Daniel Klein pursued the usual careers after majoring in philosophy at Harvard. Tom has worked with street gangs in Chicago, doctors at Blue Cross Blue Shield, and has dropped out of various divinity schools. Dan has written several novels and nonfiction books as well as jokes for comedians like Flip Wilson and Lily Tomlin. Daniel Klein lives in Massachusetts, and Tom Cathcart lives in New York City.

Praise for *Heidegger and a Hippo Walk Through Those Pearly Gates*

"Lusty peals of laughter await you everywhere in this pearly-gated gig. Hilariously, anthropologist *qua* philosopher of death Ernest Becker is a guide, glad to have his reputation for darkness lightened. Laughter, Becker said, can reflect an advanced stage of faith and grace, and that, wondrously, is what Cathcart and Klein have accomplished."
—Neil J. Elgee, MD, president, Ernest Becker Foundation

"Cathcart and Klein have a way of explaining previously difficult concepts so that anyone who can enjoy a cartoon or quip will get them. Why didn't they have these guys in my Philosophy 101 class?"
—*Cape Cod Times*

"The third in their series of small books that explain big ideas through really stupid jokes. Well, their books are a bit more than that. They're stealth intellectual weapons, so fun to read you don't notice they're also feeding you a savvy, accurate history of philosophy." —*Head Butler*

HEIDEGGER
and a HIPPO
WALK THROUGH
THOSE PEARLY GATES

Using Philosophy (and Jokes!)
to Explore Life, Death, the Afterlife,
and Everything in Between

THOMAS CATHCART
AND DANIEL KLEIN

PENGUIN BOOKS

PENGUIN BOOKS

Published by the Penguin Group

Penguin Group (USA) Inc., 375 Hudson Street, New York, New York 10014, U.S.A.
Penguin Group (Canada), 90 Eglinton Avenue East, Suite 700, Toronto,
Ontario, Canada M4P 2Y3 (a division of Pearson Penguin Canada Inc.)
Penguin Books Ltd, 80 Strand, London WC2R 0RL, England
Penguin Ireland, 25 St Stephen's Green, Dublin 2, Ireland (a division of Penguin Books Ltd)
Penguin Group (Australia), 250 Camberwell Road, Camberwell,
Victoria 3124, Australia (a division of Pearson Australia Group Pty Ltd)
Penguin Books India Pvt Ltd, 11 Community Centre, Panchsheel Park, New Delhi – 110 017, India
Penguin Group (NZ), 67 Apollo Drive, Rosedale, North Shore 0632,
New Zealand (a division of Pearson New Zealand Ltd)
Penguin Books (South Africa) (Pty) Ltd, 24 Sturdee Avenue,
Rosebank, Johannesburg 2196, South Africa

Penguin Books Ltd, Registered Offices: 80 Strand, London WC2R 0RL, England

First published in the United States of America by Viking Penguin, a member of Penguin Group (USA) Inc. 2009
Published in Penguin Books 2010

1 3 5 7 9 10 8 6 4 2

Copyright © Thomas Cathcart and Daniel M. Klein, 2009
All rights reserved

Grateful acknowledgment is made for permission to reprint excerpts from the following copyrighted works:
"Is That All There Is" by Jerry Leiber and Mike Stoller. © 1966 Sony / ATV Music Publishing LLC. All rights
administered by Sony / ATV Music Publishing LLC, 8 Music Square West, Nashville, TN 37203. All rights re-
served. Used by permission.
"Everybody Wants to Go to Heaven" by Loretta Lynn. Used by permission of Sure Fire Music Company.
"Live Like You Were Dying" words and music by Tim Nichols and Craig Wiseman. © 2004 Warner-
Tamerlane Publishing Corp. and Big Loud Shirt Industries (administered by ICG). © 2004 Big Loud Shirt /
ASCAP (administered by Big Loud Bucks) / Warner-Tamerlane Publishing Company / BMI / Bug Music, Inc. /
BMI. All rights reserved. Used by permission of Alfred Publishing Co. Inc. and Big Loud Bucks.

Page 246 constitutes an extension of this copyright page.

THE LIBRARY OF CONGRESS HAS CATALOGED THE HARDCOVER EDITION AS FOLLOWS:
Cathcart, Thomas, 1940–
Heidegger and a hippo walk through those pearly gates : using philosophy (and jokes!)
to explain life, death, the afterlife, and everything in between / by Thomas Cathcart & Daniel Klein.
p. cm.
Includes bibliographical references and index.
ISBN 978-0-670-02083-6 (hc.)
ISBN 978-0-14-311825-1 (pbk.)
1. Death.   2. Future life.   3. Immortality.   4. Death—Humor.
5. Future life—Humor.   6. Immortality—Humor.   I. Klein, Daniel M.   II. Title.
BD444.C38 2009
129—dc22   2009017128

Printed in the United States of America • Set in Fournier MT

For our philosophical mentor,
WOODY ALLEN,
whose astute phenomenological analysis
rings true to this day:
"It is impossible to experience one's own death
objectively and still carry a tune."

CONTENTS

INTRODUCTION

⁓◈⁓

Excuse us, but can you spare a moment? We're taking a survey here and we'd like to ask you a question. It'll only take a minute and we won't even ask your name, okay? So here it is:

Do you really think you're going to die?

Really and truly?

Do you really think your life is going to come to an end some day?

Take your time. No hurry to answer. Well, except for the fact that every moment that passes is one less moment in your lifetime.

If you're anything like us, you probably *don't* totally believe that the final curtain will come down one day. We can sort of grasp the fact of death in general, but in particular? Not so much. We're like the Armenian-American writer William Saroyan, who wrote in a letter to his survivors,

"Everybody has got to die, but I always believed an exception would be made in my case."

On the other hand, we can't quite get death completely out of our minds. Hard as we try to repress thoughts of our mortality, they keep popping up like those little furry heads in a Whack-a-Mole. That must be because death is one of the immutable facts of human life.

We are the only creatures who comprehend that we are going to die *and* we are also the only creatures who can imagine living forever. It's that combo that drives us crazy. Death scares the hell out of us. And a life that doesn't clearly have a destination—except over a cliff—seems devoid of meaning. This is undoubtedly why human mortality is intertwined with the fundamental questions of philosophy.

Questions like: What is the meaning of life—especially if it's all going to end one day? How should our consciousness of death affect the way we live our lives? Would life have a radically different significance if we lived forever? After a millennium or two, would we be overcome by existential boredom and long for an end to it all?

Do we have souls—and if so, do they survive our bodies? What are they made of? Is yours better than mine?

Is there another dimension of time that cuts through the cycle of birth and death? Is it possible to "live forever" by always living in the present moment?

Is Heaven a place in time and space? If not, where and when is it? And what are the odds of getting in?

These are the kinds of questions that prompted us to sign

. . . .

up for our first philosophy courses some fifty years ago. But for better or worse, we got sidetracked by professors who told us that before we could tackle the Big Questions, we had to clear up some mind-numbing technical minutiae. Questions like: Does Bertrand Russell confuse "possible necessity" with "necessary possibility"?

Whaa??

Meanwhile, time was passing and we were still going to die. Eventually, we found our way back to those Big Questions in courses in metaphysics and theology, ethics and existentialism.

But immediately another obstacle arose: honestly contemplating our own death scared us to death. We couldn't look the Reaper straight in the face without, well, fear and trembling. But we couldn't avert our eyes either. Death: you can't live with it, you can't live without it.

What's a person to do?

How about telling a joke? Hey, it couldn't hoit.

Millie accompanied her husband Maurice to the doctor's office. After he had given Maurice a full checkup, the doctor called Millie into his office alone. He said, "Maurice is suffering from a serious disease brought on by extreme stress. If you don't do the following, your husband will die. Each morning, wake him up gently with a big kiss, then fix him a healthy breakfast. Be pleasant at all times and make sure he is always in a good mood. Cook him only his favorite meals and allow him to relax after eating. Don't burden him with any chores, and don't discuss your problems with him; it will only make his stress worse. Don't argue with him, even if he criticizes you or makes fun of you. Try to relax him in the evening by giving him massages. Encourage him to watch all the sports he can on TV, even if it means missing your favorite programs. And most important, every evening after dinner do whatever it takes to satisfy his every whim. If you can do all of this, every day, for the next six months, I think Maurice will regain his health completely."

On the way home, Maurice asked Millie: "What did the doctor say?"

"He said you're going to die."

Somehow hearing about mortality from Millie makes it more bearable. Jokes are funny that way: they can make a devastating point while defusing anxiety at the same time. That's why there are so many jokes about sex and death—both of them scare the pants off us.

Happily, we happen to know a lot of jokes. In fact, we once discovered that jokes are a neat way to clarify general philosophical ideas, and we even wrote a book about that. So could jokes also illuminate philosophical concepts about life and death, Being and Non-Being, eternal souls and eternal damnation while at the same time alleviating our death-angst?

You betcha!

And that's a good thing, because the time is nigh (we've both recently attained our biblically allotted three score and ten) for us to take an unflinching look at Death and what the big thinkers have to say about it, so we're going to need all the laughs we can get. We'll be prying open all the coffin lids on this issue, looking not only at the Big D but also at its prequel, Life, and its sequel, the Sweet Hereafter. We'll be looking for clues.

We'll start off by taking a look at the fabulous ways civilized societies have come up with to deny our mortality, especially through that perennial diehard, organized religion. In particular, we'll check out Freud's theory of how we create religions—as well as havoc—in order to support our illusion of immortality.

Next we'll check in with some nineteenth-century philosophers from northern European countries. (Why aren't there any philosophers on the Italian Riviera who write about death?) We'll visit with that melancholy Dane, Søren Kierkegaard, who thought the only way to transcend our death-anxiety is to go *through* it. For Kierkegaard, all of our attempts to suppress our thoughts of death are counterproductive. The one way to get in touch with the eternal is to take the anxiety of nothingness into ourselves. Say it ain't so, Sø!

Then we'll see what that grim German philosopher Arthur Schopenhauer has to say. He virtually patented the concept of *Weltschmerz* (free translation: "The world makes me want to hurl"). You might think his attitude toward death would be super-schmerzy, but Schopenhauer, no fan of Life, regarded Death with utter apathy. He wrote that the "death of an individual is of absolutely no consequence" and therefore "our deaths should be . . . a matter of indifference to us."[1]

Indifference to death? That's not real helpful, Artie, and the needle on our angst-meter is going crazy. Quick, we need a good indifference-to-death gag.

So Ole died, and his wife Lena went to the local paper to put a notice in the obituaries. The gentleman at the counter, after offering his condolences, asked Lena what she would like to say about Ole.

Lena said: "You just put 'Ole died.' "

Perplexed, the man said, "That's it? There must be something more you'd like to say about Ole. You lived together fifty years, you have children and grandchildren. Besides, if it's money you're worried about, you should know that the first five words are free."

"Okay," Lena said. "Put down, 'Ole died. Boat for sale.' "

No look at philosophies of death would be complete without a visit to the twentieth-century existentialists, who saw not-existing as a companion piece to existing—sort of like a matched set. So we'll check in on Martin Heidegger and Jean-Paul Sartre, who tried to look unflinchingly at deadness. Heidegger claimed that we actually *need* the anxiety of death to keep us from falling into "everydayness," a state in which we're only half alive, living with a deadening illusion. And Sartre told us to consider the alternative: the only beings that don't have death anxiety are those that are already dead as doornails—like doornails, for example. Get real, they admonish us. We'd like to, but first we have to stop shaking.

So we'll take a short break from all this heavy philosophizing to examine a popular form of death-denial: reassuring ourselves that we will live on in the hearts of those who knew us. This strategy assumes a certain sentimentality on the part of our loved ones that may or may not be, you know, *there*.

Old Sol Bloom lay dying in his bed, when he suddenly smelled the aroma of his favorite strudel wafting up the stairs. He gathered his remaining strength and lifted himself from the bed. Leaning against the wall, he slowly made his way out of the bedroom and forced himself down the stairs, gripping the railing with both hands. With labored breath, he leaned against the door frame, gazing into the kitchen.

If it weren't for the pain in his chest, he would have thought he was already in Heaven. There, spread out on paper towels on the kitchen table, were literally hundreds of pieces of his favorite pastry. Sol smiled; this was one final act of love from his devoted wife, Sophie, seeing to it that he left this world a happy man.

With quivering hand he reached for a piece of the strudel. Suddenly he felt the slap of a spatula.

"Stay out of those," Sophie said. "They're for *after*."

From here to profundity, as we grapple with twentieth-century theologian Paul Tillich's answer to the question, "*When* is eternity?" (Turns out it's now.) But "now" keeps shifting to "then." So how about *now*? Slippery stuff.

We feel the need for something more solid to hang onto, so we'll inspect the ancient Greek arguments for the immortality of the soul. But first we need to get clear on what we mean by a soul, how it differs from a mind, how both mind and soul differ from a body, and how all three differ from a zombie.

After laying the Greeks to rest, so to speak, we'll look at Heaven and other destination spots for the afterlife.

Fred and Clyde had had many conversations over the years about the afterlife. They agreed that whoever died first would try to contact the other and tell him what Heaven was like.

Fred was the first to pass on. A year went by. One day the phone rang, and when Clyde answered, it was Fred!

"Is that really you, Fred?" he asked.

"You bet, Clyde. It's really me."

"Great to hear from you! I thought you'd forgotten. So tell me! What's it like there?"

"Well, you won't believe this, Clyde. It's absolutely wonderful! We've got the most delicious veggies from the lushest fields you have ever seen. We get to sleep in every morning, have a fabulous breakfast, and then make love the rest of the morning. After a nutritious lunch, we go out in the fields and make love some more. Then it's time for a gourmet dinner and some more love-making until bedtime."

"Omigod!" said Clyde. "Heaven sounds fabulous!"

"Heaven?" said Fred. "I'm a rabbit in Arizona."

Then we'll wrap it all up with a peek at near-death experiences, séances, suicide, and some wild new ideas on how to avoid death altogether.

Hold it right there, guys. This is starting to sound like much ado about Nothingness.

Who said that?

Me, over here. Daryl Frumkin from down the block. I was walking my dog Binx when I heard you guys talking. And all I've got to say is this death thing is pretty simple, isn't it? First you're alive, then you're dead. End of story.

Really, Mr. Frumkin? That's all there is to it? So can we ask you a question?

Do you really think you're going to die?

· I ·

Dead!
Whatcha Gonna Do
About It?

Surely There Must Be Some Mistake

Uh, Daryl, we're still waiting for an answer here. Do you really think you're going to die?

Well, sure, I know everybody dies. Frank Sinatra's gone. So is Norman Mailer. Not to mention Napoleon, Harry Truman, Genghis Khan, and my wife's Aunt Edna. So logically it stands to reason that one day I will be dead too. I know that as sure as I know apples fall down instead of up.

Good, Daryl. Well said. But let's be perfectly clear here, we're not talking about your twenty-first-century scientific mind that calls 'em the way it sees 'em. No, we're talking about your regular, sitting-here-on-our-porch consciousness. Right now, do you really believe that your days are numbered, that each moment that ticks by is subtracting from your allotted moments as a living human being? That when you reach your that's-all-she-wrote moment, you will cease to exist in every conceivable sense of existence?

Huh? You're mumbling, Daryl. We know it's a daunting question, but perhaps we can help you out here.

Our guess is that, in your heart of hearts, you don't really believe you're going to die. And the reason for that is that you are a civilized human being. That's nothing to be ashamed of—at least not yet. We human beings have one heck of a problem accepting and incorporating this obvious fact into our consciousness. So what we do on a moment-to-moment, day-to-day basis is *deny* our mortality. Actually, we usually do this fairly easily with all the help we get from the social structures and customs of whatever civilization we happen to live in.

In his masterwork, *The Denial of Death,* the twentieth-century cultural anthropologist Ernest Becker wrote that even though we know *objectively* that we are mortal, we cook up all kinds of schemes to escape this devastating truth. (Becker died just two months prior to being awarded the Pulitzer Prize for his book—an untimely death if ever there was one.)

Why we desire to deny our mortality is pretty obvious: the prospect of death is terrifying! It brings on the ultimate angst. It gives us the fantods to face the fact that we are only here for a short time, and when we are gone, we're gone for eternity. How can we enjoy life with the clock ticking so loudly in our ear?

According to Becker, the only way most of us deal with this situation is delusion—in fact, the Big Delusion. The B.D. is the basic human drive—way more basic than the sex drive, he says—and it gives rise to "immortality systems," nonra-

tional belief structures that give us a way to believe we're immortal. There's the ever-popular strategy of identifying ourselves with a tribe, race, or nation that lives on into the indefinite future, with us somehow a part of it. Then there's the immortality-through-art system, in which the artist foresees her work enduring forever, and therefore herself immortalized too—in the pantheon of Great Artists or, at the very least, as a signature at the bottom of a sunset landscape propped up in a corner of her grandchildren's attic.

Then there are the top-of-the-market immortality systems enshrined in the world's religions, ranging from living on as part of the cosmic energy in the East to sailing off to be with Jesus in the West. At a less lofty level, there is the immortality-through-wealth system. This one provides us with a nifty life goal to wake up to every morning: go get more money. That way we don't have to think about the Final Bottom Line.

Wealth also admits us to a tribe that will live on: the exclusive club of movers and shakers. There's even a bonus—we can pass along a piece of ourselves, our moolah, to the next generation.

But *caveat emptor!* (Or, if you're not from ancient Rome, "Let the buyer beware!")

When Bob found out he was going to inherit a fortune after his sickly father died, he decided he needed a woman to enjoy it with. So one evening he went to a singles' bar where he spotted the most beautiful woman he had ever seen.

Her natural beauty took his breath away. "I may look like just

"I should have bought more crap."

an ordinary guy," he said as he walked up to her, "but in just a week or two my father will die, and I'll inherit twenty million dollars."

Impressed, the woman went home with him that evening. Three days later, she became his stepmother.

The go-for-the-bucks route offers another popular way of simulating immortality: donate to an immortal institution, hopefully one that will emblazon your name on the front of a building, or cut out the middleman and just build a monument to yourself.

But before you assume that your vow of poverty (or at least of a middle-income salary) will get you off the hook, think again, says Becker. You're still probably striving for some earthly goal that lulls you into believing you're here forever. Say you strive to be "hip" or "saintly" or "style-setting"—it's the same deal. You're still buying into the Big Delusion that you're outsmarting the Reaper by adopting a role that transcends your puny, scary individuality and makes you "bigger than life" . . . and death.

We sustain these various delusions simply by being civilized, according to Becker. Virtually every civilization has evolved a shared immortality system. In fact, these systems are the basic function of a culture. Without them, we'd all go wacko with death-angst and we wouldn't be able to keep our civilization humming along. We'd return to the law of the jungle. Denial of death is civilization's survival strategy!

It's easier to sustain a delusion if you have it in common

with others in your culture, or better yet, right inside your own house. Consider the shared delusion of Clara and her husband.

Clara went to a psychiatrist and said, "Doctor, you've got to do something about my husband—he thinks he's a refrigerator!"

"I wouldn't worry too much about it," the doctor replied. "Lots of people have harmless delusions. It will pass."

"But you don't understand," Clara insisted. "He sleeps with his mouth open, and the little light keeps me awake."

Unfortunately, immortality systems make us behave badly. When we identify with one immortality system and invest it with ultimate personal meaning, we have this nasty problem of coming up against other folks with different systems. We often see this in the clash of world religions, and it presents a major problem: all our immortality systems can't be right, so the others' must be wrong.

But civilization has provided a remedy for that too: *Kill the bastards!* Once they are dead, they won't be a threat to our own sense of immortality. Hey, works for us.

A lot of ink has been spilt over all the blood that has been spilt in the name of a particular religious doctrine and its specific immortality system. Christopher Hitchens's *God Is Not Great: How Religion Poisons Everything,* the bible of the "new atheist" movement,

*"You picked the wrong religion, period.
I'm not going to argue about it."*

has an exhaustive inventory of all the crimes against humanity committed to maintain the primacy of our own religion. But surrealist comedian Emo Phillips has a story that pretty much sums up the situation.

I was walking across a bridge one day, and I saw a man standing on the edge, about to jump off. So I ran over and said, "Stop! Don't do it!"

"Why shouldn't I?" he said.

"Well, there's so much to live for!"

"Like what?"

"Well . . . are you religious?"

He said yes.

I said, "Me too! See? We've got lots in common already, so let's talk this thing through. Are you Christian or Buddhist?"

"Christian."

"Me too! Are you Catholic or Protestant?"

"Protestant."

"Me too! Are you Episcopalian or Baptist?"

"Baptist."

"Wow! Me too! Are you Baptist Church of God or Baptist Church of the Lord?"

"Baptist Church of God!"

"Me too! Are you original Baptist Church of God, or are you reformed Baptist Church of God?"

"Reformed Baptist Church of God!"

"Me too! Are you Reformed Baptist Church of God,

reformation of 1879, or Reformed Baptist Church of God, reformation of 1915?"

He said, "Reformed Baptist Church of God, reformation of 1915!"

I said, "Die, heretic scum," and pushed him off.

Phillips has an even shorter version (if you're running out of time):

Probably the toughest time in anyone's life is when you have to murder a loved one because they're the devil.

ONE DEEP THINKER'S ILLUSION
IS ANOTHER'S WISDOM

Becker's contention that denial of death is mankind's Big Delusion comes with an impressive pedigree. In his short treatise "The Future of an Illusion," the father of psychoanalysis and mother of the unconscious, Sigmund Freud, named the fear of death as one of the major factors that drive humans to create and defend the illusion of gods and religion. Because we are helpless before the prospect of death, our unconscious invents a father-figure-in-the-sky to help us cope. Conveniently, Sky Daddy rewards good behavior too, so, Siggy says, we have a compelling reason to resist our most antisocial instincts—"incest, cannibalism, lust for killing," that sort of thing. But most importantly, the Ultimate Father Figure alleviates our fear of death by providing life everlasting for those who conform to society's demands.

In short, Freud thinks belief in God and in God's promise of eternal life is a cultural fairy tale designed to help us escape the specter of death.

Never one to shy away from contradictions, Freud later cooked up the *Todtriebe,* or drive *toward* death (often mistranslated as the "death instinct"). Freud's original hypothesis had been that the pleasure principle, *Eros*—the drive to maximize life, love, pleasure, and productivity—was humankind's prime motive. But as Freud grew older he looked down upon humanity, and, lo, something else seemed to be in play here, something not so pretty. Like all that war and mayhem couldn't be accounted for by just Eros. Enter the Death Drive.

At its most benign, the Death Drive expresses itself in our need to withdraw from stimulation and pursue peace and quiet; it's a kind of dress rehearsal for death. Freud referred to this as the "Nirvana principle," the need to "conduct the restlessness of life into the stability of the inorganic." Be your own compost. Anyone who has watched bowling on TV from a BarcaLounger can relate.

So all this means we should turn our *Todtriebe* inward, right? No way, says Freud. This is one powerful drive, the Todtriebe, and once let out of its cage it turns into a monster: it won't be satisfied with simply watching *Bowling for Dollars;* it's got an appetite for masochism and suicide.

So we should turn our Death Drive *outward*, right? *Nein!* says Siggy. That way lie murder, mayhem, and war. Yikes! What's a poor schlub to do?

See a shrink, says Freud. The goal of therapy—and of living—is to harmonize the Death Drive and Eros, get them into balance.

JUNG AT HEART

Just because the whole God-religion-eternal-hereafter package comes from our unconscious doesn't necessarily mean that it's all hog swill, argued Freud's onetime disciple, the Swiss analytical psychologist Carl Gustav Jung. Maybe our unconscious is *wiser* than our conscious mind. Maybe what Sigmund calls unconscious fabrication is really unconscious confirmation. Maybe we don't make up religions, we discover them inside us. And just maybe, as the unconscious psyche gets passed on from generation to generation, it evolves on its own, getting smarter while our conscious minds merely continue to limp along.

What is really going on, says Carl Gustav, is that religions speak for the psyche by providing symbols that come "from the heart." The reason these symbols have revelatory power is that they are products of our deep, unconscious mind, a storehouse of instinctual wisdom that is accessible to our conscious mind only through dreams, cultural myths, and religions. It is when the conscious mind gets out of touch with

*"Look, making you happy is out of the question,
but I can give you a compelling narrative for your misery."*

this deeper psyche—becomes alienated from it—that we develop neurotic symptoms, like getting depressed as hell by the ultimate meaninglessness of it all.

PSYCHED!

Had Jung lived just a little longer—he died in 1961—he might have added psychedelics to his list of pathways to one's deeper, more enlightened psyche. Magic mushroom and LSD trips provided many a sixties seeker with transcendental insights into what appeared—at least at the time—to be a Higher Reality.

Yet to our knowledge, none of these drug-induced states produced an account that is either as astounding or as clear as Jill Bolte Taylor's meticulous observations while watching herself undergo a massive stroke. In 1996, this Harvard neuroscientist watched in fascination as the left hemisphere of her brain shut down. In the process, Dr. Taylor came to know a spiritual reality that Jung only dreamed of.

Taylor explains that the right hemisphere of the brain processes what is going on for us at the present moment. It thinks in pictures, taking all of the sights and sounds and smells occurring for us *right now* and putting them together in a whole. In our right brain, we are "perfect, whole, and beautiful." We experience ourselves as an "energy being" that is connected to all the energy in the universe and to the energy of the whole human family.

By contrast, our left brain is linear and methodical. It takes the present moment and picks out details, connects them to past learning, and projects future possibilities. It thinks in language, not pictures, and one of the things it says is "I am." It experiences the self as separate from the energy flow around it and separate from other human beings. It is the function of this left brain that Taylor largely lost during her stroke.

As her left brain shut down, she experienced herself as boundaryless and at one with all the energy in the universe. She felt peaceful and euphoric. At the same time, her left brain—her *anxious* brain—would intermittently kick in with the message, "You are in danger of dying! You must get help!" But getting help without the sustained assistance of her left brain was nearly impossible. Even after she managed to phone for help, as she tried to explain her situation, all she could do was bark like a dog.

Later, in the hospital, she experienced the world around her as chaos and noise, but then suddenly felt her spirit soar through a "sea of euphoria."

Taylor's conclusion? The world is full of loving, peaceful people who can "step to the right of their left brain." We are at once beings who are "the life-force power of the universe" and also beings who are separate

from the world and separate from others. And most significantly, to some degree we can choose to be in either
place at any given time.[1]

What Taylor experienced in her right brain was what Jung
called the deep, unconscious source of religious experience.
Jung had only speculated about where this experience origi-
nates; Taylor pinpointed its location. Taylor's right-brain experience exploded her left brain's constructs of time and
space. Her experience was transcendental: she was part of the
Immortal All.

Jung says that the unconscious psyche is not only instinctu-
ally aware of the fact that we die, but actually accepts this fact.
The psyche prepares itself for death, usually many years before it happens. While our rational, conscious mind sees death
as an anxiety-provoking, grim finale, our psyche—our right
brain?—accepts it.

*Jeez, I guess there is more to death than coffin nails, isn't
there?*

Yes, Daryl, and we're afraid it only gets scarier.

{ 2 }

Let Your Angst Be Your Umbrella

Daryl, we've got some bad news and some good news. Which do you want first?

I'll take the bad news.

Okay, here it is—this is going to get a whole lot more anxious-making.

Great. So what's the good news?

The good news is that after we finish this book, we're taking our wives on a vacation to the south of France!

But first back to Becker. He says that in the end neither psychology nor organized religion can provide us with a sanctuary from the life-is-meaningless-and-then-you-die problem. Neither of those can rid us of the anxiety of facing death, or its flip side, the anxiety of facing a life that is finite and can never satisfy our yearning for infinity.

Those anxieties are part of the human condition, whether we like it or not (personally, we don't). Add to them the fact that we are the only creatures that pay death taxes, and what we have is a tinderbox of angst.

Not to worry; Becker says there is a way to authentically accept our mortality and transcend it in a manner that puts us in touch with a Higher Reality without the need to make trouble with anybody else's immortality system. To understand this route, we have to reach way back to the mid-nineteenth century, long before Freud or Jung, to the Danish philosopher and religious thinker Søren Kierkegaard, the father of existentialism.

Most of us would rather skip over the anxiety of contemplating death and jump immediately into some happily-ever-after immortality system like, say, a front-row lawn chair in Heaven. But that hippity-hop route is a highway to Nowhere according to Becker and his inspiration, Kierkegaard. If we skip the step of confronting Death head on and of hanging in there while we experience the prospect of Eternal Nothingness, if we deny ourselves the full load of dread and terror that accompanies living in the face of "Nevermore," then we'll also miss out on our only chance to experience transcendence. That, says Søren, is because angst is our ultimate teacher!

Hold it right there, guys! This Dane sounds like a nut job! For starters, it's a well-known fact that you learn things better if you're in a good mood than in a bad mood. And let me tell you, I'm getting in a real bad mood listening to this stuff.

We know whereof you speak, Daryl. We couldn't help but notice that you are quaking in your skin, tears running down your

FREE-FLOATING ANXIETY
(MAGNIFIED 200,000,000 TIMES)

cheeks as you focus on the incontrovertible fact that Life is short and Death is sure. And we have to admit, it doesn't exactly feel like the best time for a learning experience. But let's give Søren a chance to make his case. You know, out of respect for the dead?

First we need to do some catch-up on the human condition. In *The Concept of Dread* and *The Sickness unto Death* (it was those upbeat titles that made S.K. such a hot seller in Denmark), Kierkegaard arrived at the meaning of anxiety and despair through a mix of philosophy and psychological introspection. But the psychological problems Søren was interested in weren't the kind that spring from one's personal history—like, say, that your mother always preferred your brother and that your dad thought you were a wuss—but rather the issues we all have as a result of being human and mortal. In fact, we suspect that if Kierkegaard were alive today, he might think the neuroses your corner psychotherapist treats are mere substitutes for our real issue: being responsible for living a meaningful life on the edge of the abyss of death.

Time out, bozos! I know all about therapy. I saw a shrink myself for a while because of my anger-management problem. And it turned out you're right—it was all because my mother just adored my brother Skippy, and Dad, well, you know . . . I'd been bottling up that anger for years. And it had absolutely nothing to do with death or the abyss or any of that mumbo jumbo.

Maybe, Daryl. But Kierkegaard might say that the whole issue of needing maternal love is just a smoke screen. There are anxieties and depressions that just come with the territory of being a human person, no matter how much your mother loved you or

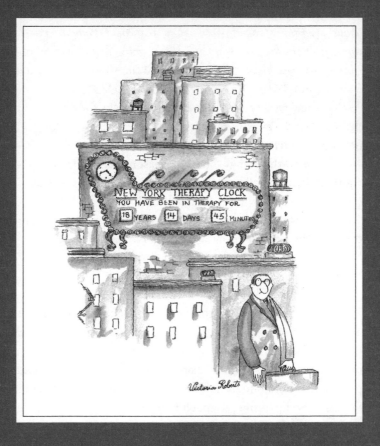

your father put you down. And those anxieties and depressions are
the Mother of all the particular anxieties and depressions you
groan about on the couch. According to S.K., all your anxiety
about everything comes way before the couch complaints—it
comes from the fact that you know you're going to die. And maybe
working out your issues about Mom and Skippy and Pops is just a
way to distract yourself from your real issue—the Big D!

If garden-variety neuroses are really masks for our fear of
death, it might explain why psychotherapy takes so long. It
never gets down to the real issue: deathiness.

Of course there may be *other* reasons why normal psychotherapy takes so long. Comedian Ronnie Shakes tells us:

**After twelve years of therapy my psychiatrist said something
that brought tears to my eyes. He said, "No hablo inglés."**

A Streetcar Named Despair

For Kierkegaard, rock-bottom human anxiety and despair, as
compared to *neurotic* anxiety and despair, have us coming and
going. Some of us are overwhelmed by too much possibility:
our time-limited selves can't handle the unlimited options that
present themselves to us in both our everyday lives and in our
fantasies. So little time, so much I *might* do.

Let's tune in on an anxious mortal dithering in the face of
too much possibility:

Will I ever be as great a kisser as Brad Pitt? Should I give up my
law practice and try to make it as a street performer? What

should I do with my life? Should I let my inner woman out? How about my inner Rambo?

Should I try to be both Supermom *and* run a construction company? Should I have an affair with the postman and risk my happy home life? Or should I deny myself an affair and go to my grave unfulfilled?

Do I dare to eat a peach? A Mars bar? A magic mushroom?

Am I a loser?

If I had an infinite amount of time, I could try an infinite number of these options. But there's something about death that puts the kibosh on my personal possibilities. Since I've got one time-limited life, I don't want to waste forty years of it trying to be as good a kisser as Brad Pitt. Or, even worse, *dithering* about whether to try to become as good a kisser as Brad Pitt. Because while I'm dithering, the clock is running down. *Tick, tock, tick, tock. Is that your final answer?*

JUST DO IT

It was exactly these dilemmas that led those latter-day existentialists, the merchandisers at the Nike Corporation, to coin their trademark leap of faith: **Just Do It.**

But the Nike folks ran into some cultural boundaries in Africa. They filmed a commercial for hiking shoes in Kenya using Samburu tribesmen. The camera zooms in on one of these tribesmen as he intones a few words in his native Maa just as the "Just Do It" slogan flashes on the screen. When it played on American television, an anthropologist from the University of Cincinnati noted that what the guy actually was saying was, "I don't want these! I want big shoes!"

An embarrassed Nike spokesperson admitted they had difficulty finding a Maa equivalent of "Just Do It," so they just did it with whatever the tribesman felt like saying. Nonetheless, from a Kierkegaardian point of view, the man is a fine example of someone who does not dither about his options.

Oy! The pressure of being accountable for a finite life is enough to drive a person around the bend. And according to Kierkegaard, our Who-am-I? and What-can-I-be? puzzlements can push us over the edge of anxiety and even make us schizophrenic, like the guy who walked into a psychiatrist's office and said, "I have an identity problem . . . and so do I."

One tempting way out of Kierkegaard's existential hell of overwhelming what-to-be options is to *simply close down.* To avoid the angst of too much possibility, I shut myself off completely from the world.

Our anxious mortal again:

First I numb myself. It seems like a good anti-anxiety strategy, and in the short term, it is. But now I'm feeling isolated, disconnected from my family, my friends, my dog Moishe, my John Deere riding mower, the Knights of Columbus. And I can't seem to find my way back! I can't snap out of it. "Just Do It" just doesn't do it when my strategy is to not do anything. What started out as a way

The Inescapable Self

The self is one's chief interest.

to escape my fear of inadequacy has me feeling way more inadequate. Back when I felt bad because I wasn't as good a kisser as Brad Pitt? Man, those were the good old days! Since I numbed out, I don't feel alive enough to be a *person,* let alone a kisser.

But I still feel the pain of being me. I've only got two choices left: stop the pain permanently—say, by overdosing on trans fats—or try some strategic loopholes.

LOOPY LOOPHOLES

Here's one escape clause that seems promising on the surface, Søren says: *stay inside myself, but make it a virtue!*

Let's tune in again on our anxious mortal:

Like, I am so aware. I see the big picture and I'm not bothered by the details. Life is a parade, and I have a great seat. And, oh, God, it's like so good *not* to be part of the parade. Now I go to the Knights of Columbus meetings, but I keep a certain ironic distance. As a matter of fact, I find it mildly amusing.

So why, you may ask, am I ordering my third martini while the sun's still out?

Here's another of Søren's tricky tickets out of despair: *lose myself in the trivialities of life.* Tranquilize myself by getting caught up in "everydayness." *Pas de problème!*

Here's our Anxious Man again:

I'm feeling really good. I've got my BlackBerry loaded. Every moment of my day is accounted for: 6:00–6:15, first latte; 6:15–6:45, treadmill; 6:45–7:00, email & Facebook; 7:00–8:00, drive to therapy while listening to my Deepak audiobook; 8:00–8:50, dig into my assertiveness problem with my shrink, Dr. Gonzales; 9:00, sit down at my desk and check my in-box . . .

Wow! It's a full life! A 24/7 merry-go-round.

But wait one second. What's that in my rearview mirror? It looks like a guy in a black bathrobe riding a pale horse. An off-duty mounted policeman? Omigod, it's Mr. D. himself! Funny, *he* wasn't in my BlackBerry.

One more Kierkegaardian escape strategy: *Bravely throw myself into acts of "defiant self-creation." Make something of myself.*

Load up my bedside table with self-help books by Wayne Dyer, Eckhart Tolle, Marianne Williamson. Think positive thoughts! Dare to dream the impossible dream! Visualize great goals! Harness the secret powers of the law of attraction! Then my life will have meaning, and that meaning will transcend death. I will be immortal. Like Lawrence Luellen. A name that will live on in eternity.

You don't remember Larry?! The inventor of the Dixie Cup?

Lily Tomlin points out one of the practical problems of trying to make something of yourself:

I always wanted to be somebody. Now I see that I should have been more specific.

So, Daryl, you're probably wondering, what if you're all mixed up? What if you've got so many conflicting life strategies going that you don't know who you are most of the time?

The Self at a Gathering

The Self as Something to Be Improved

Like, what if you're both hyper and depressed? Like the manic-depressive who went on vacation and sent a note back to his psychiatrist: "Having a wonderful time. Wish I were dead."

No, that's not what I'm thinking at all! I'm still thinking this Kierkegaard is a few Danishes short of a coffee break. What's more, he's depressing the hell out of me.

Okay, Daryl! Here comes the Final Answer—Søren's clincher.

There *is* a way out that doesn't come up against the dead ends of autoanesthesia, solipsistic confinement, busy-bee-ing, or self-aggrandizement. But, we've gotta warn you, it's not exactly a walk in the park.

Angst itself is the way out! Pretty cool, eh, Daryl? It's only when we dare to experience the full anxiety of knowing that life doesn't go on forever that we can experience transcendence and get in touch with the infinite. To use an analogy from gestalt psychology,[1] Non-Being is the necessary ground for the figure of Being to make itself known to us. It's only when we're willing to let go of all of our illusions and admit that we are lost and helpless and terrified that we will be free of ourselves and our false securities and ready for what Kierkegaard calls "the leap of faith."

We can't resist telling this golden oldie just one more time. (The devil makes us do it.) It perfectly nails Kierkegaard's point about one man's readiness to take that leap of faith.

A man stumbles into a deep well and plummets a hundred feet before grasping a spindly root, stopping his fall. His grip grows weaker and weaker, and in his desperation he cries out, "Is there anybody up there?"

He looks up, and all he can see is a circle of sky. Suddenly the clouds part and a beam of bright light shines down on him. A deep voice thunders, "I, the Lord, am here. Let go of the root, and I will save you."

The man thinks for a moment and then yells, "Is there anybody else up there?"

So, Daryl, does Kierkegaard speak to your death-angst? Daryl? Daryl? Where'd he disappear to?

Death—The Way to Go!

Too bad Daryl's not here, because do we have some cheerful news for him. And it's straight from the mouth of the nineteenth-century German philosopher Arthur Schopenhauer. For Artie, there's no reason to have anxiety about death. That's because death is the ultimate aim and purpose of life. It's like the ultimate fulfillment!

Huh? What kind of crazy talk is that?

Oh, there you are, Daryl, curled up in the fetal position under the porch. Well, take a deep breath, my friend. We know this isn't the answer you were hoping for. It is *kind of a downer at first blush, but Schopey is an acquired taste.*

As it happens, the Schopster did have several interesting ideas about death on his mind. One thing he meant is that life is a constant process of dying. The past, when you really think about it, is just a repository of death, a heap of no-longer-existing events—gone forever, irretrievable, dead as a doornail (or as a dormouse, depending on where you shop for similes). Artie flips the old feel-good aphorism "Today is the first day of the rest of your life" to "Today is the last day of your death, so far."

THE PAST AS PRESENT

Nonetheless, says Schopey, we cling to life because we have this perverted "will-to-live," which—contrary to our best interests—keeps us from embracing our true destiny, death. It's views like this that kept Schopenhauer from getting invited to Oktoberfests.

THE PERVERTED WILL-TO-LIVE
ON DEATH ROW

An Italian, a Frenchman, and an American are about to be executed. They're told they can have whatever they want for their last meal.

Tony replies, "A nice bowl of linguini with clam sauce." He enjoys his plate of pasta and is duly executed.

Next, it's Pierre's turn. "I'd like a nice hot bowl of bouillabaisse." He relishes each spoonful, and is executed.

Finally, it's Bill's turn. He thinks for a minute, then says, "I'd like a nice bowl of fresh strawberries."

"Strawberries?" says the warden. "They're out of season."

"No problem. I'll wait."

"Happy fortieth. I'll take the muscle tone in your upper arms,
the girlish timbre of your voice, your amazing tolerance
for caffeine, and your ability to digest French fries.
The rest of you can stay."

*Hold it right there, guys! Schopenhauer's calling my love of life a "*perverted will-to-live*"? He's the one with the perverted view, I tell you! He's a few bread crumbs short of a schnitzel, and you guys are just eating it up.*

Be patient, Daryl. You've got to maintain an open mind on these things. Sure, Schopey had an unusual philosophical take on things. And there's no getting away from the fact that he's got a terminal case of Weltschmerz. But if it's uplift you want, why don't you go watch Extreme Makeover?

Truth to tell, Schopenhauer went on to top himself with an even bigger downer. He said that death is a welcome relief from life. He cited Lord Byron as his ally in dissing life's meager pleasures:

> Count o'er the joys thine hours have seen,
> Count o'er the days from anguish free,
> And know, whatever thou hast been,
> 'Tis something better not to be.

In one passage, the Schopmeister even went so far as to conclude that, all life's heartbreaks considered, 'tis something better *never to have lived at all!*

Sam and Joe, two elderly gents, were talking on a park bench.

Said Sam, "Oy. All my life, one trouble after another. A business that went bankrupt, a sickly wife, a thief for a son. Sometimes I think I'd be better off dead."

Joe: "I know what you mean, Sam."

Sam: "Better yet, I wish I'd never been born."

Joe: "Yeah, but who has such luck? Maybe one in ten thousand?"

But hold on—Schopenhauer insists he's no pessimist. Just because he says life is a constant source of suffering and frustration, we shouldn't jump to the conclusion that he was of the Life-Sucks-and-Then-You-Die school of philosophy.

Au contraire, Artie was more Buddhist than pessimist. He had read the Buddhist scriptures in an early European translation, and agreed with the Buddha that all existence is suffering. But, also like the Buddha, he didn't think it ultimately mattered, because the ordinary world is just an illusion. The only thing that's *really* real is what he called "Will," by which he meant the blind, irrational, aimless Force that keeps the whole shebang—and everything in it—going. In short, what's to be pessimistic about? The stuff that's always getting our knickers in a knot isn't real anyhow.

For Schopenhauer, the problem with life in this world of illusion is that my *individual* will gets split off from the *transcendental* Will with a capital *W* and starts to have a life of its own. First day out of the box, it gets attached to the illusory stuff of the everyday world. Schopenhauer says these illusions include *everything,* from my career goals to my patriotism to my devotion to my particular religion. These attachments pit *my* individual will against *your* individual will, and therein lies the source of all the world's suffering.

Of course, one of the big things we get attached to is our

own continued survival: we have this crazy will-to-live. How self-destructive can we get, eh, Daryl? Wanting to live only makes us suffer more! So we need to let go, resign ourselves to the futility of the world of appearances, and accept the fact that both life and death are unreal.

Still unconvinced that Schopenhauer's not a downer? That's because you haven't heard the good news: Will-itself never dies! It has no "death event," because events occur only in the world of appearance. Will (capital W) is indestructible.

Blues gone now, Daryl?

Actually, Daryl, we do feel a little better. Kind of. Like, we can sort of get the feel of these quasi-mystical takes on Life and Death. At least on Tuesdays, Thursdays, and Saturdays. It's only the days in between that they sound loony.

Throughout the entire history of philosophy, thinkers have been trying to figure out the relationship between Being and Non-Being, life and death. These fundamentals boggle the mind. But on days when we have a lot of wonder and awe going for us, we can get a sense of what they mean, and on those days we see "through a glass darkly" that you can't have Being without Non-Being—or vice versa. And further, that Being and Non-Being are in constant tension with one another. It's the basic Cosmic Battle. So if Schopenhauer sides in this battle with the force of Being that he calls Will—well, maybe he is some sort of wacky optimist after all.

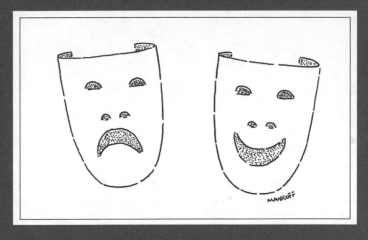

"I don't get it." *"You never get it."*

{ 4 }

Heideggerty-Dog, Ziggity-Boom, What You Do to Me

Listen up, Daryl, because this next guy has a weird way with words.

The twentieth-century German existentialist Martin Heidegger is probably the most quoted modern philosopher on the subject of death. Terrific! If we only knew what he was saying.

> To think Being itself explicitly requires disregarding Being to the extent that it is only grounded and interpreted in terms of beings and for beings as their ground, as in all metaphysics.[1]

Got it? We especially like his throwaway line, "as in all metaphysics." Here's another:

> Time is not a thing, thus nothing which is, and yet it remains constant in its passing away with-

out being something temporal like the beings in
time.[2]

What more can we say? Except that we hope his philosophy is more intelligible in German, a proposition he seems to
hint at in another quote:

The German language speaks Being, while all the
others merely speak of Being.[3]

But then again, he is also on record as saying,

Making itself intelligible is suicide for philosophy.[4]

Thanks for that, Marty—you gave us back our self-esteem.
*We need all the help we can get here, Daryl. Got any clues
what he's talking about?*
Huh?
Actually there is a reason why Heidegger plays such a
prominent role in the contemporary philosophy of death, and
not only because a cover-to-cover reading of his masterwork,
Being and Time, is the existential approximation of a near-
death experience. No, Heidegger's big contribution to the
phil. of D is his injunction to confront death head-on in
order to live authentically—to live honestly, realizing what
life really is. Without death-consciousness, we're only half
alive. According to one scholar, Marty actually put this very
clearly:

> If I take death into my life, acknowledge it, and
> face it squarely, I will free myself from the anxiety
> of death and the pettiness of life—and only then
> will I be free to become myself.[5]

Heidi stresses the fact that only a human being is aware of
his mortality, unlike, say, a pussycat. The latter may scratch
and bite to avoid being eaten by my dog Moishe, but she is *not
conscious* of the Big Void that awaits her if Moishe prevails.
Awareness of mortality is thus unique and fundamental to the
human condition, which happens to be the condition our condition is in.

Yet most of us manage to keep this awareness cranked
down and dim. We live in *denial of death,* and in Heidegger's
opinion, that's not living at all. We can't fully realize life unless we are conscious of our upcoming demise. Consider this
queen of denial:

The priest was warning his listeners about the suddenness of
death. "Before another day is ended," he thundered, "somebody
in this parish may die."

Seated in the front row was a little old Irishwoman who
laughed out loud.

Irritated, the priest said, "What's so funny?"

"Well!" said the old lady, "I'm not a member of this parish."

"Thank goodness you're here—
I can't accomplish anything unless I have a deadline."

Memento Mori—The Ultimate
Weapon Against Denial

Memento mori is one of those catchy alliterations that first caught on when they still spoke Latin in Rome. We both flunked conversational Latin, but we're told it means "Remember you are mortal!" or, in a more recent translation, "Remember you are mortal, goombah!"

In ancient times, the phrase was repeated by a slave boy who walked behind a war hero returning to the streets of Rome in a triumphant march. Its purpose was to serve as a reminder that "Okay, you're on top of the world today, but like all of us, the day will come when you are dog meat!" As a Great Leveler, *memento mori* traditionally carries more weight than, say, "Hey, he still has to pull on his socks in the morning," or "Yeah, well, even the Queen has to sit when she goes to the loo."

In other situations and in other eras, the M.M. was more an *aide-mémoire* to seize the day, to "eat and drink, for tomorrow we die" (as the prophet Isaiah put it), and, in Christian times, to live virtuously because the Day of Judgment (the first Tuesday following your demise) is nigh.

In the arts, pictorial, literary, and musical, *memento mori* images serve the same mnemonic purpose. Think Frans Hals's *Youth with a Skull* or Holbein's *The Dance of Death* (skeletons doing the hokey-pokey over a gravesite); Hamlet's tête-à-tête with Yorick's skull; and

Saint-Saëns's *Danse Macabre*. And then there's a piece of installation art that until recently greeted shoppers at Jones's Junkyard in Great Barrington, Massachusetts: a skeleton arrayed in a glass case with the legend, "As you are now, I once was; as I am now, you will be."

It's enough to give you the fantods.

Okay, it's a no-no to deny death—we can dig that, so to speak. But leave it to Heidegger to push his idea one step further. He goes on to say that the anxiety of anticipating death, contrary to interfering with life, brings an "unshakable joy."

Hold it right there! You've got another wack job on your hands, guys! Is he actually saying, "Yippee, skippy, I will cease to exist forevermore—hot damn!"?

Truth to tell, Daryl, Marty actually does have something interesting on his mind.

Look at it this way: Say you're Kevin Garnett and this is Game 7 of the NBA Finals. You're going to play with way more intensity, way more energy, way more *life,* than in one of those dreary Thursday night midseason games in Charlotte. Heidegger called the latter "everydayness," and he put it down as the ultimate drag. So let's face it squarely, Daryl, this—right here, right now—*is* Game 7 of the Finals, and what a joy it is to be here!

For Heidegger, the worst possible news would be that our souls are immortal. That would condemn us to a never-ending string of those Thursday night games in Charlotte.

HEIDEGGER GOES COUNTRY

Heidegger's precept to always live in the shadow of death has been echoed by many deep thinkers. Mahatma Gandhi said, "Live as if you were going to die tomorrow. Learn as if you were to live forever." And none other than the prematurely departed movie star James Dean said, "Dream as if you'll live forever. Live as if you'll die today."

But our favorite iteration is found in the lyrics of Tim McGraw's country and western hit "Live Like You Were Dying." The song tells the story of a man in his forties who is told by his doctor that he has a very short time to live. In the chorus, the man says to his friend:

> I went sky diving
> I went Rocky Mountain climbing
> I went 2.7 seconds on a bull named Fumanchu
> And I loved deeper and I spoke sweeter
> And I gave forgiveness I'd been denying
> And he said, *Someday I hope you get the chance*
> *To live like you were dying.*

HEIDEGGER GOES HOLLYWOOD

In the Rob Reiner comedy *The Bucket List*, two terminally ill sexagenarians make a break from the cancer ward to fulfill their lists of things-to-do-before-they-die. Those lists include getting tattoos, visiting the Great Wall of China, race car driving, skydiving (apparently an activity on everybody's final wish list but ours), scaling the Himalayas, and finding the perfect woman. Along the way, the pair intone the wisdom they acquire facing death head-on, gems like, "Never pass up a bathroom, never waste a hard-on, and *never* trust a fart."

A spiritual quest it is not, but nonetheless it *is* living smack in the face of death. To be sure, *The Bucket List* does not dramatize men who are living *as if* they are about to die; they really *are* about to die. Yet to Heidegger, this would be a nondistinction: we are *all* about to die—exactly *when* is just a quibble.

QUIBBLE

Doctor: I have some good news and some bad news.

Patient: What's the good news?

Doctor: The tests you took showed that you have twenty-four hours to live.

Patient: That's the good news? What's the bad news?

Doctor: I forgot to call you yesterday.

QUIBBLE, QUIBBLE

Marty goes to Doctor Lewis for a check-up. After extensive tests the doctor tells him, "I'm afraid I have some bad news for you, Marty. You only have six months to live."

Marty is dumbstruck. After a while he says, "That's terrible, doctor. And I must admit to you that right now I can't afford to pay your bill."

"Okay," says Dr. Lewis, "I'll give you a year to live."

The French existentialist Jean-Paul Sartre read Heidegger (in six straight days at a table in Les Deux Magots, according to Sartre's waiter) and did his own riff on the existential significance of death. Sartre said the meaning of death is that "the for-itself is changed forever into an in-itself that has slipped entirely into the past."[6]

Any questions? The French are so much more *suaviloquent* than the rest of us, is it not so? Turns out the "for-itself" is Jean-Paul's term for human consciousness, which he tells us is called "for-itself" because it is not a *thing.* If it were a thing, it would be an "in-itself."

Why can't these philosophers speak plain English?

For one thing, Daryl, Sartre was French.

Yeah, well, he still sounds a few Folies short of a Bergère.

What Sartre means is that human beings have no "essence," no predetermined purpose like, say, a rubber ducky does. "In themselves" human beings are *nothing;* rubber duckies, on the other hand, are quite something, as anyone who's ever been stuck in a bathtub for three hours can attest. Sartre thinks a key difference between human beings and the duckies is that we humans invent our own essence by choosing to be what we want to be. There are other differences too, of course. But we humans are *for ourselves,* self-created, rather than *in ourselves,* created for a fixed purpose.

Or at least that's the way we ought to be—always freely reinventing ourselves. But, alas, most of us have this nasty habit of wanting to be a *thing*—no, not a table-thing or a wall-lamp-thing or a bathtub-thing, but a human-role-thing, like dissolving our identity into our profession or our nationality or our reputation on the golf course. In this way, we slip into inauthenticity, a kind of living death, like Sartre's famous waiter, who thinks that waiterhood actually defines his essence. Silly *garçon.* He fails to see that the possibility of freedom—the possibility to transcend what he's become—is always there.

Until he *really* dies, that is. At that point, we all become things. Then we do have a stamped-on essence: to wit, the essence of dead meat.

LOSS OF FOR-ITSELFNESS

"The turkeys in your frozen-food section seem so small. Do they get any bigger?"

"No, ma'am, they're dead."

Spin Your Own Immortality

Listen, guys, my angst meter just went on red alert, so how about a little lighten-up break? Like, have you guys heard any good jokes lately?

Geez, Daryl, we're not sure the existentialists would approve of blowing off angst just when it's building up steam. But we have to agree, a little break wouldn't hurt. We'll slide down Ernest Becker's list of immortality systems to one that has an all too obvious shortcoming, but also just happens to be teeming with some of our favorite gags. We're talking about the so-called immortality that comes from being remembered by our survivors.

First, a couple of words from the sages:

"Why should I care about posterity? What's posterity ever done for me?"

That one's from Groucho Marx. And here's a topper from his philosophical godson, Woody Allen:

"I don't want to live on in the hearts of my countrymen; I want to live on in my apartment."

The sages' salient point is that living on in the hearts and minds of our survivors fails to meet a crucial criterion for what most of us want to mean by "immortality": it lacks eternal ego consciousness. You may be living on in others' minds, but you won't have one of your own.

But one thing Becker fails to address is the relative handiness of living eternally through memorials. Unlike, say, assuring yourself a place in Heaven, here-on-earth commemorations have a user-friendly system and a ready-made infrastructure. Memorializing yourself these days is easy by Googling, say, sculptors "statue on stallion" "Bayonne, NJ."

A bigger-than-life statue of yourself in the middle of a park is always a good way to achieve this kind of immortality. All you have to do is call your local sculptor and deposit a few mill in the city coffers. A building or boulevard bearing your name does the trick too. And a lengthy biography by a Yale professor, complete with photographs and thirty pages of endnotes, is also neat. But unfortunately there is only so much public park space, so many boulevards, and so many willing Yale professors, not to mention the fact that after burial costs, few of us will have millions in disposable income left over for public monuments.

That leaves the rest of us with obituaries, eulogies, high-production-value funerals, last wills and testaments, and last words as memorabilia media. Apart from these mini-marks in the sand, about all we can expect to get embedded in the minds and hearts of those who knew us—at least, beyond our immediate family and closest friends—is something like, "That Daryl, he sure was a cut-up." And the uncomfortable truth is that within a generation that probably will be reduced to, "Didn't there used to be a guy named Daryl around here somewhere?"

Gags, guys! I'm not feeling any uplift yet!

Hang in there, Daryl. It's on the way. But you can't have a gag without a setup.

Anyway, a fascinating obituary or a few moving, heartfelt eulogies or a well-turned last phrase have much to be said for them. Principally, they give our survivors a hook on which to hang their memories of us. Therefore you may want to consider a few practical ways we actually can shape this little piece of eternity.

Consider the pitfalls of a poorly planned memorial service:

Stanley Goldfarb died and his relatives and the congregation gathered for an evening of prayers and mourning. When the time came for the congregation to offer eulogies, no one stirred. After waiting several minutes, the rabbi became vexed; he reminded them that it was their duty to find something good to say in Goldfarb's memory. "Someone must have something nice to say about him!" After another period of silence, an old man rose in the back and stammered: "I'll say this for old Stanley. His brother, Morris, was worse."

Few of us get to be spectators at our own funerals, but that doesn't stop many maximum control types from making detailed preparations for them, including ghostwriting (so to speak) their own eulogies. They may have a point.

A careful planner of one's own funeral is also aware of common gravesite mishaps, starting with settling for a discount mortician.

Mickey has just passed away and his wife, Judy, goes to the mortuary. As soon as Judy sees her husband she starts crying. An attendant tries to comfort her. Through her tears Judy explains that Mickey is wearing a black suit, and he always wanted to be buried in a blue suit. The attendant explains that they always put the bodies in a black suit as standard procedure, but he'll see what he can do.

The next day, when Judy returns to the mortuary to have one last moment with Mickey, she smiles through her tears— Mickey is now wearing a blue suit. Judy asks the attendant, "How did you manage to get hold of that nice blue suit?"

"Well, yesterday, after you left, a man about your husband's size was brought in, and he was wearing a blue suit. His wife was very upset, as he had always wanted to be buried in a black suit," the attendant replied. "After that, it was simply a matter of swapping the heads around."

"He was a man of simple tastes—
baked macaroni, steamed cabbage, wax beans,
boiled onions, and corn fritters."

And speaking of burial get-ups, some special economic questions need to be addressed here, like, if you are buried in a rented tuxedo, at what point do you own it?

A first-rate funeral needs to be choreographed as flawlessly as a production of *Swan Lake*. One glitch and that's all the attendees will remember about you, instead of your years of devoted service to the Keep Bayonne Green Association.

Jack had passed away and his funeral service was being held at Woodlawn Cemetery. Jennifer, his wife for over forty years, had tears in her eyes. At the end of the service, as the coffin was being wheeled out, the trolley accidentally bumped into the door frame. To everyone's total shock, they heard a faint moaning coming from inside the coffin. They quickly opened it and found Jack alive. Wonder of wonders—a miracle if ever there was one.

Jenny and Jack lived together for ten more years and then Jack died. The ceremony was again held at Woodlawn. At the end of the service, as the coffin was being wheeled out on the trolley, Jenny shouted, "Watch out for that door frame!"

Another major consideration for a memorable funeral is turnout. Empty pews translate into low-buzz immortality. If at all possible, schedule your funeral for an uneventful day.

Joe gets a ticket to the Super Bowl from his company, but when he gets there, his seat is in the last row in the corner of the stadium. Halfway through the first quarter, Joe sees through his binoculars an empty seat ten rows off the field, right on the fifty-yard line. He decides to take a chance, and makes his way to the empty seat.

As he sits down, Joe says to the guy sitting next to him, "Excuse me, is anybody sitting here?"

The guy says, "No."

Joe says, "This is incredible! Who in their right mind would have a seat like this for the Super Bowl and not use it?"

The guy says, "Well, actually, the seat belongs to me. I was supposed to come with my wife, but she passed away. This is the first Super Bowl we haven't seen together since we got married in 1967."

Joe says, "That's really sad. But couldn't you find anyone to take the seat? A friend, or a close relative?"

The guy says, "No, they're all at the funeral."

DEAD AND IN COLOR!

When it comes to immortalizing a life story, a significant problem with obituaries, eulogies, last words, and even headstones is durability. In fact, it has been demonstrated that the average headstone lasts roughly a millennium less than the average fruitcake. Fortunately, the digital world has changed all that.

Enter Hollywood Forever, a thriving California graveyard that guarantees eternal life in the form of a eulogy posted eternally on the Net. No, really, we're not kidding. And it's not just some cookie-cutter, run-of-the-mill eulogy either, but a full-color movie memoir with snappy cuts and really gorgeous background music, like Barbra Streisand warbling "Memories."

These professionally produced films are not only screened at the funeral service and go home with each mourner in an attractive DVD sleeve, they can be punched up on each of the many video kiosks that dot Hollywood Forever Cemetery. And most significantly, these biopics are written by and star the deceased—prior to shedding his or her mortal coil, of course. HFC customers get to direct their own immortality!

A fundamental philosophical question is raised by all of this, in fact, the prime question of historiography: What are the proper role and scope of history-recording? Who gets mentioned and who not? If a grocery clerk dies in the forest, did he exist?

The philosophically minded historian Howard Zinn has argued that histories that only dwell on kings and presidents, or generals and explorers, leave out 99 percent of the population. In his seminal work *A People's History of the United States*, he rights the balance by including such ordinary people as Plough Jogger, a farmer and participant in Shays' Rebellion, and Harriet Hanson, a Lowell mill worker. So maybe Hollywood Forever has it right after all.

One option for immortality in the minds and bank accounts of survivors is leaving loot behind. In this way, every time your grandniece, Tiffany, buys a new pair of snakeskin pumps, she will be thinking, "Thank you, Uncle Daryl!" or possibly, "Thank you for dying, Uncle Daryl!" Whichever. Your name lives on.

Of course, as with every contractual agreement, slip-ups are unavoidable.

"Hey, Bob, remember when you and I went fishing up north nine months ago and the car broke down in that thunderstorm and we wound up spending the night at that farm owned by that gorgeous widow? Remember?"

"Yeah."

"You remember the gorgeous widow?"

"Yeah."

"And she had that big, fabulous house and we slept in the guest room, and the next morning we got in the car and headed north and went fishing—you remember?"

"Yeah."

"Well, nine months later I got a letter from her attorney."

"Oh?"

"Did you happen to get up in the middle of the night and go pay her a visit?"

"I did. Yes."

"And did you happen to use my name instead of telling her your name?"

"I'm sorry. I did. Why do you ask?"

"She just died and left me everything."

Undoubtedly the most cost-effective route to immortality in the memories of your survivors is a pithy and memorable final utterance. For some reason, the general populace gives these last words more weight than, say, something funny you once said at a party after your third martini.

Here are a few of our all-time favorites:

> I am about to—or I am going to—die: either expression is correct.
>
> Dominique Bouhours, French grammarian, d. 1702

> LSD, 100 micrograms.
>
> Aldous Huxley (to his wife, who then injected him), d. 1963

> Leave the shower curtain on the inside of the tub.
>
> Hotel magnate Conrad Hilton, d. 1979.

> *A truck!*
>
> Comedian Emo Phillips's grandfather.

> Don't let it end like this. Tell them I said something.
>
> Pancho Villa, Mexican revolutionary, d. 1923

Philosophers, on the other hand, seem to lack a certain *panache* in their final moments:

> I owe Asclepius a rooster.
>
> Socrates, the Number One philosopher
> of all time, d. 399 B.C.

> I desire to go to Hell and not to Heaven. In the former I shall enjoy the company of popes, kings and princes, while in the latter are only beggars, monks, and apostles.
>
> Niccolò Machiavelli, political philosopher, d. 1527

> It's my turn to take a leap into the darkness!
>
> English philosopher Thomas Hobbes, d. 1679

> Go on, get out! Last words are for fools who haven't said enough.
>
> Karl Marx, d. 1883

But alas, Daryl, once you're gone, there's little you can do to keep your memory alive or, for that matter, to keep it cute. On the up side, what you don't hear won't hurt you.

A man walks out of his office during a thundershower and, lo and behold, there's an empty taxi right there! He hops in and remarks to the driver how lucky he is to get a taxi in such weather. The cabbie turns to him and says, "You obviously have perfect timing . . . just like Sheldon."

"Who?"

"Sheldon Schwartz. Now *that* was a guy who did everything right. He was the luckiest guy in the world. Probably the closest thing to human perfection this planet has ever seen. For example, Sheldon always managed to get a parking spot right in front of the door, no matter where he went."

"Ahhh, come on! You're exaggerating. Nobody's that lucky!" says the passenger.

"Sheldon was," says the cabbie. "Not only was he lucky, but he was an amazing athlete. He easily could have been a golf or tennis pro. He had a voice that would shame Placido Domingo into giving up opera! He was handsome and sophisticated, more than Cary Grant. Boy, you should have seen him in a tuxedo! He was a prime physical specimen—big and tall and strong. He was also a terrific businessman. Everything he touched turned to gold. And boy! what a wonderful card player!"

"Oh, come on!" said the passenger. "You're making this up!"

"No. I'm not. Sheldon had other gifts too. Like, he always knew how to please a woman. He was brilliant also. There was nothing he didn't know, nothing he couldn't fix. Not like me. I change a fuse, and I short out the entire neighborhood. And boy, did he know how to tell a story! He was the life of every party!"

"Wow, he sounds incredible. How did you know this Sheldon?" the passenger says.

"Well, I never actually met him," admits the cabbie.

"Then how do you know so much about him?" the passenger asks.

"After he died, I married his wife."

Okay, Daryl, had your fill of anxiety-soothing gags now?

Anxiety-soothing? Now I'm more depressed!

That's okay. Now we can get down to some neat philosophical takes on Eternity!

· II ·

Eternity
When You Least
Expect It

✦

Is Eternity out there in the Great Beyond?
Or is it lurking right here in the neighborhood?
If so, who has time for it?

{ 6 }

The Eternal Now

Don't be such a sourpuss, Daryl. It's not only unbecoming, it's unnecessary, because great news is on the way! And it's happening right now.

Because here's one that boggles the mind from here to eternity: Eternity is *Now*!

Let's start with the basics. It is *always* now. Right *now*, for example. You, Daryl, getting up off the porch with your pooper scooper and slouching over to that spot on the lawn where Binx made his little mess, now doing your scooper thing, depositing it in your neighbor's mailbox, now climbing back onto the porch and cracking open a can of Bud Light. "Now" follows you the whole way. Oops, it's now again. Or, rather, it's *still* now. And it always will be!

This puts the idea of Eternal Life into a whole new framework, like, *Eternity is right now,* not after death when you thought it was.

Major twentieth-century philosophers Ludwig Wittgenstein and Paul Tillich had interesting takes on the concept of the Eternal Now. Ludwig had his take in two different points in space, Vienna, Austria, and Cambridge, England; Paul's were in Frankfurt, Germany, and Cambridge, Massachusetts.

Tillich, an existentialist Christian theologian, believed that eternal life is not life that goes on and on with no end in sight, like *Law and Order*. To Tillich, as to Heidegger, that would be an image of Hell. Rather, the eternal is right here *in every moment of time*. It is a *dimension* of time that cuts into time. The eternal is present *now* as the Eternal Now.

Unlike, say, rocks, human beings can look down on time and see the big picture, including the end, and thereby experience anxiety and despair. That's the bad news. But Tillich is an existentialist, and like Kierkegaard, he sees the fact that we are creatures capable of such anxiety as good news.

How so? Because it indicates that unlike rocks, human beings are only partially *in* time. We also have one foot *outside* of time, or else we wouldn't be able to look down on our situation and see it in its finitude and experience the anxiety of death. For example, we can use the term "life span" and know whereof we speak.

TIME AND ETERNITY: THE INTERSECTION

So *eternal life* for Tillich is not endless life in the "sweet bye and bye"; it is life lived in the Eternal Now. The trouble is that we fall out of touch with the eternal dimension; we become

*"When it's eternity here,
it's still early morning on the West Coast."*

"separated" from it and fall into despair, but it is there just the same. The trick is to try to reach that transcendental perspective. *Like right now!*

To understand what Tillich is getting at, we have to jump out of linear time as we experience it, the before-and-after, see-you-next-Saturday kind of time that we normally think of. Instead, we have to try to get our minds around the idea of Time itself—time the dimension, time the organizing principle. For help, we again turn to the contemporary philosopher Allen Stewart Konigsberg, or, as he is known to everyone but his mother, Woody Allen. Says Königsberg, **"Time is nature's way of keeping everything from happening at once."**

KEEPING IN TIME

Jumping "outside of time" should not be confused with "messing with the sequence of time," the latter currently being a popular storytelling device used in such films as *Memento* and *Mulholland Drive*, and in the gag riddle that goes like this:

Q: What happens when you play a country song backward?

A: You get your girl back, you get your truck back, you may even get your dog back.

Reversing the time sequence, even though it can open interesting questions about cause and effect, and about how we construct our memories, still remains within the structure of linear time. Jumping-out-of-time views the entire dimension of time as, well, a dimension.

It is not often that we get to quote the analytic philosopher Ludwig Josef Johann Wittgenstein alongside Woody Allen and Paul Tillich, but now seems as good a time as any. In his seminal work, the *Tractatus Logico-Philosophicus*, L.J.J.W. says, **"If we take eternity to mean not infinite temporal duration, but timelessness, then eternal life belongs to those who live in the present."**[1]

By "timelessness," Ludwig seems to mean, "apart from or outside of the dimension of time." The "now" we always exist in is timeless—it is not a "part" of time. Wittgenstein's conclusion that eternal life belongs to people who live in the present has a surprisingly New Age feel to it, more often associated with people like Baba Ram Dass (known to *his* mother as Dickie Alpert). In the early 1970s, everybody who was anybody made time to read Baba's tract *Be Here Now*, a guide to post-hallucinogenic spiritual consciousness. The title says it all; it is a guide to living in the present.

Psychologically and spiritually, getting in touch with the Eternal Now can be problematic. We tend either to dwell on the past or anticipate the future and end up never getting around to simply being here now.

Thinkers and gurus in the East have approached this

difficulty in a practical way: they have devised rituals to lead us into existing in the moment. Meditation, yoga, and tai chi are techniques for emptying the mind and simply Being.

Is Now Over Yet?

Things get really confusing when we try to set a time limit on "now." Zeno, of Achilles-races-the-tortoise paradox fame,[2] argued that time could be divided into an infinite number of portions. That sure doesn't leave much time for "now." Or, as the contemporary British playwright and wit Michael Frayn put it, **"Ah, *now*! That odd time—the oddest time of all times; the time it always is . . . by the time we've reach the 'w' of 'now' the 'n' is ancient history."**

Fortunately, we have a more practical idea of 'now' from that dependable pragmatist, the late-nineteenth-century American philosopher and psychologist William James. He called now "the specious present," by which he meant the false sense we have that "now" has some content, albeit slight, and some duration, albeit short, when in fact the present doesn't exist at all. It's merely the boundary line where the past meets the future, neither of which can really be said to exist either, at least not now. In other words, "now" is a subjective construct that we use to mark our experience of time.

This raises one of philosophy's perennial questions:

"Nothing happens next. This is it."

Is the experience of a length of time relative to the experiencer, especially if one of the experiencers happens to be a pig?

A guy is driving down the road and sees a farmer lifting a pig up under an apple tree. Each time the farmer lifts the pig up, it bites off an apple. The guy in the car stops and asks what's going on.

The farmer says, "I'm feeding my pig."

The guy in the car says, "If you just shook the tree and let the pig eat the apples off the ground, wouldn't that save a lot of time?"

And the farmer says, "What's time to a pig?"

* * *

The mystic poet William Blake wrote,

> To see a World in a grain of sand,
> And a Heaven in a wild flower,
> Hold Infinity in the palm of your hand,
> And Eternity in an hour.
> Pants pressed while you wait.

Just kidding—we added that last line.

You know, I get your point this time, guys. In fact, I've always planned on living in the present someday. But you guys are supposed to be philosophers, right?

. . . .

Sort of, Daryl. More like superannuated students of philoso-phy. What's your point?

So you're telling me that none of these big-time serious thinkers just looks at death and says it sucks, plain and simple?

Funny you should ask.

After all the philosophical attitudes that somehow accom-modate death—often making it the logical and desirable bookend to birth—and all the theological and cultural para-digms that make it a mere step to a grander condition, there is something refreshing about the position of just being pissed off that life has to end. *Supremely pissed off!*

But come to think of it, we *can't* think of a single major philosopher or world religion that subscribes to the position that death is nothing more than a dreadful prospect, the worst possible cheat imaginable. To be sure, it would be counterin-tuitive to presume that religion would take this attitude—rec-onciliation, in one form or another, is basic to religions' appeal. They wouldn't stay in business long if they told us that death is final and it sucks.

But one would think that at least one of those truth-seekers known as philosophers would face the end squarely and just plain abhor it. Not so. Raging against death appears to be the business of poets:

> Do not go gentle into that good night,
> Old age should burn and rave at close of day;
> Rage, rage against the dying of the light.
>
> Dylan Thomas

· III ·

Immortality
the Old-fashioned Way—
On the Soul Train

∙✦∙

Do we have an immortal soul?
Where is it?
Can you sell it on eBay?

Plato, the Godfather of Soul

Where do you guys live—in a cave? Death isn't The End, it's the Beginning! Haven't you ever heard of the immortality of the soul?

Of course we've heard of the immortal soul, Daryl. It's just that we've never seen one. Not only that, but Ernest Becker places the idea of immortality of the soul high on his hit list of delusionary systems.

But before we slam the coffin shut on this idea, let's nail down what a soul is. We don't want any surprises down the road, like if we find out that the part of ourselves that survives death is some part we don't even like.

The ancient Greeks are a good place to start. Apparently these guys in togas had a lot of time on their hands to ponder such things as the soul. (Who was cooking supper while the guys were schmoozing is a question for Feminist Ethics.) The Greeks were dualists—not to be confused with duelists, which was more of a Roman thing; they thought the soul and the body are two totally different kinds of beings. One of the earliest Greek philosophers, Thales, saw the soul as simply the force that *moves* the body. He had acutely observed that one of the big differences between a dead body and a live one is that the former doesn't move, at least not on a level surface. *Ipso facto,* something must leave the body when it dies—like, say, the motor. Other pre-Socratic philosophers noticed that dead people don't seem to know anything anymore and added *knowing* to the functions of the soul. Still others noticed that dead people don't seem to see or hear either and added the function of *perceiving*.

But it was Plato who put together a comprehensive picture of the soul. He said there are three parts of the soul: Reason, Spirit (or Will), and the Appetites. Reason—wouldn't you know?—is the highest part, the part that is able to commune with the eternal Ideas or Forms, like Beauty, Wisdom, and the Triangle—that is, the Ideal Triangle, the triangle "Form" from which all earthly, imperfect triangles get their triangularity. (Don't ask.)

The Will is one of the irrational parts of the soul, but, on the upside, it is nobler than the Appetites. Properly harnessed, the Will inclines toward Reason. The Appetites, on the other hand, resist reason, pulling us down toward our sensuous desires, which spells trouble with a capital *T* (i.e., Trouble).

Philosopher W. Allen points out that **"the soul embraces the nobler aspirations, like poetry and philosophy, while the body has all the fun."** But Plato counters that while the Appetites do have all the fun, they're actually part of the *soul*. This is one of the key differences in the philosophies of Plato and Allen.

For Plato, the ultimate goal of the soul is to strip off its sensuous nature and move toward knowledge of the Forms; immortality is reserved for the rational part only. In other words, contemplating the triangle trumps sex, drugs, and rock 'n' roll.

He prefers a triangle to sex? This guy sounds a few Doric columns short of a Parthenon.

We urge you to withhold judgment until you've seen this triangle, Daryl. It isn't any old triangle, it's the Ideal Triangle.

Aristotle had a slightly different take on the soul, but his conclusion was similar. He divided the soul into the *vegetative soul*, which causes the mechanical and chemical changes that we share with animals and vegetables; the *animal soul*, which creates the locomotion and experiences the sensations that we share only with animals; and *reason*, which we don't share with any animal or vegetable. Like, try reasoning with your cat. Or your carrot.

Ari further divided reason into *passive reason* (perception) and *active reason* (thinking, conceiving, visualizing Aphrodite in your bedroom, that sort of thing). For Aristotle, it is active reason that's the immortal part of the soul.

"Dear, there's someone here to collect your soul."

The Greek notion of the soul as an *entity* gave Wally Scott the idea of selling his on TradeMe, New Zealand's equivalent of eBay, in 2008. Of course, the idea of selling one's soul is at least as old as Faust, but Scott's innovation lay in seeing that there is a mass market for souls, and not solely the devil. Bidding for Scott's soul reached $189.

Several philosophical questions, of course, needed to be addressed. First was the issue of how bidders could be certain of the condition of Scott's soul at the time of sale. Scott maintained that it was in "pretty good nick" with the exception of a "rough patch" when he reached the legal drinking age.

Then there was the question of what rights were implied in the passage of the title from Scott to the buyer. Scott's lawyer maintained that the mere fact of owning Scott's soul would not entitle the buyer to own or control *him*—a tricky distinction, we thought.

Finally, there was the question of whether TradeMe rules should permit the sale of something as intangible as a soul. In the end, TradeMe ruled that because a Deed of Soul Ownership would change hands, they would permit the sale.

The folks at eBay were more skeptical. In 2001, bidding for Alan Burtle's soul had reached $400 when eBay pulled the plug, saying that nothing tangible would be transferred. By "tangible," they meant something like a

vintage Pokémon or a Beanie Babies collection, two of
their most popularly traded items.

The question of immortality of the soul would not have come
up in ancient Israel. Unlike the Greeks, the Hebrews didn't
see human beings as divided into two separate parts, body and
soul. The soul in the Hebrew Bible refers to the whole person.
Human beings don't *have* souls; they *are* souls. And they
don't *have* bodies; they *are* bodies, living bodies.[1] How's that?
What's the difference, then, between a dead body and a living
body, you may ask. Well, the Bible isn't real clear on this, but
it seems to be something like the difference between a live battery and a dead battery. It's not that the dead battery is missing a part; it's just missing *pizzazz*. What it's missing is *life*.

I'M ALL FOR YOU, BODY AND . . . WHATEVER
Paradoxically, Edward Heyman, the lyricist who
penned the jazz classic, "Body and Soul," was of the
Hebrew persuasion. The rumor that Heyman's rabbi in-
formed the songwriter that he was making a false distinction and should call the song "Body and Body" is
unsubstantiated.

Same deal in the New Testament. To "lose your soul" is
simply to lose your life. "What does it profit a man if he gains

the whole world and loses his soul?"[2] means simply "What does it profit a man if he gains the whole world and loses his life?"

PROFIT AND LOSS

If we take the New Testament at its word, it seems to suggest a cost-benefit analysis of "gaining whole world" vs. "losing soul." As with all questions of valuation, it depends on the evaluator.

A lawyer woke up one night and found his bedroom awash in red light and foul with a sulfurous stench, and there at the foot of the bed was someone he recognized instantly as Satan.

Satan smiled and said, "Mr. Jones, if you wish, I will give you untold wealth and all the women you want, plus fame and a long life. How about it?"

The lawyer's eyes narrowed. "What's the catch?"

Satan replied, "In exchange for all of that, I will take your immortal soul."

And the lawyer said, "Come on. What's the real catch?"

In ancient Indian philosophy, the ātman, or Self, totally transcends most of the functions the Greeks included in their conception of the soul. In fact, the seat of thoughts, emotions, etc., which was an integral part of the Greek notion of the soul, is regarded by the Indian sages as a body part, albeit the "*subtle* body." But this isn't even the biggest difference between the Greek and Indian notions. For the Hindu sages, the Self isn't something we own individually, like a Harley or a Panama hat: it's the universal stuff that pervades everything in the universe, as in the ancient parable of the Hindu who asks the hotdog vendor to make him one with everything.

Both Plato and Aristotle talked about a universal Reason that underlies our individual reason, but they also maintained the idea of an *individual* soul that survives death. By contrast, in Indian thought—Hinduism, Buddhism, and Jainism—to become immortal means to transcend our individuality and "step off the wheel of birth and death."

Oh, yeah? What about reincarnation, then? I always thought that sounded like a good deal. Like I used to be Napoleon, then I was Daryl, next I may be a bunny rabbit.

You're not alone, Daryl. A lot of Westerners think that reincarnation is the Eastern version of immortality of the soul. But no way, Sanjay! First of all, Buddhists, the chief source of the Western idea of reincarnation, don't even believe in the soul. Their concept of reincarnation is the passing of a flame from one candle to another. No *self* gets transferred in the deal, because there's no self to transfer.

Secondly, reincarnation isn't all it's cracked up to be. Sure, our subtle body gets to keep on truckin', but it's still truckin' on the same old gravel road. Reincarnation merely subjects our psyche to another round of struggle and purification on the way to finally realizing our true and universal Self. To get there, we must step *off* the gravel road of multiple deaths and reincarnations, become one with the universal Self, and ride on eternally in an Off Road Vehicle.

In fact, reincarnation is just an extension of the law of karma. People who do evil become evil—in this life and beyond. People who do good become good—in this life and beyond. But what we become in our next life shouldn't be viewed as a reward or punishment; the purpose of reincarnation is to give us an opportunity to evolve.

CREATIVE EVOLUTION

"Do you believe in reincarnation?" a golfer asked a friend during a round at the local municipal course.

"Why, yes, I do," said the buddy.

"Well, how do you want to return to earth?"

"I want to come back as a lesbian."

"What! Why?"

"I still want to make love to women, but I want to hit from the shorter tees."

But some of us have been going in the wrong direction. According to a Hindu text, the *Garuda Purana*, the murderer of a Brahmin will come back with tuberculosis. (Sorry, Brahmin-killers.) The killer of a cow doesn't fare much better: he or she returns as a humpbacked imbecile. Remember that when you're pouring ketchup on your next Quarter Pounder. And the murderer of a virgin? A leper, of course. Figures.

The New Agers have adopted some of the more exotic features of belief in reincarnation. A website called Reincarnation Station provides a short quiz to determine what you'll likely come back as. We're not saying who's who, but one of us will be back as a really cute panda; the other, as a rat.

MEANWHILE, BACK IN THE WEST . . .

Many of the functions of the soul described by the pre-Socratics and Plato and Aristotle are what we would now call functions of the mind: locomotion, knowing, perceiving, desiring, willing, reasoning. In fact, the Greek word for soul is *psyche,* a word we now use to mean "mind." Psychology, the modern study of the psyche, is the study of the mind, not the study of the soul.

So what do we Westerners have in mind when we refer to a "mind"? Does it provide any clues to the immortality question? Like how does it differ from that part of our *body* that's located in our skull—the brain? If the soul is just the mind and the mind is just the brain, there goes any shot at

*"I imagine serenity's pretty much the same,
one season to the next?"*

immortality. A term you often hear around the ICU is illustrative: *braindead*.

In the seventeenth century, the father of modern Western philosophy, René Descartes, put forth the dualistic view that Mind and Matter (which includes the brain) are two altogether different kinds of beings that occupy different realms with different rules, with no point in common. But that raises a question: If they don't overlap in some way—if they exist in their own separate spheres—how can it be that matter can cause changes in the mind and the mind can cause changes in the material world? For example, physical objects apparently cause our perceptions of them, and our "will" seems to cause parts of our body to move. And then there's the business of certain chemical substances that can cause big-time changes in our minds, like visions of plasticine porters with looking-glass ties.

DUALISM IN A NUTSHELL

What is Mind?

No Matter.

What is Body?

Never Mind.

So what exactly is the link between Body and Mind?

Another seventeenth-century philosopher, the German rationalist Gottfried Wilhelm von Leibniz, maintained that Mind and Matter *don't* actually get into each other's knickers. He said they operate in parallel, like two synchronized but separate clocks. Each goes forward in its own realm, and the changes in one are merely *associated* with changes in the other because this harmony was preestablished by God. Thanks for that info, G.W.V.L., but you may want to lay off the mind-altering substances for a while.

The nineteenth-century Darwinist T. H. Huxley said the mind is merely a *side effect* of bodily functions, an "epiphenomenon" like shadows on the ground. Physical brain states can cause changes in mental states, said the epiphenomenalists, but mental states can't cause anything, even other mental states. So while our bodies, brains included, go about their business, our minds simply show the pictures.

The "logical behaviorists," including the twentieth-century British philosopher Gilbert Ryle, took it a step further. Ryle ridiculed Descartes's view that mind and body are two different kinds of beings, with the mind somehow "inhabiting" the body. Ryle called that idea "the ghost in the machine." He said Descartes had led us in a centuries-long detour trying to define what sort of *entity* this ghost is, when in fact the mind is not an entity at all. To have a mind isn't to possess a certain *thing;* it's simply to have certain capacities and dispositions. We go around thinking that mental states, such as beliefs and desires, *cause* our behavior. In fact, our behavior is caused by dispositions to behave in certain ways, and our mental states simply reflect those dispositions. That doesn't seem to leave anything to be immortal; it's hard to picture immortal capacities and dispositions. But then again, who knows? Lots of us find it hard to picture an immortal mind or soul of any kind.

The development of computer technology has raised interesting questions in the mind-body debate. In 1950, A. M. Turing, one of the founders of computer science and a celebrated British World War II codebreaker, asked the question whether it is theoretically possible for a large enough computer to answer questions in such a way as to fool us into thinking that it is a human being—like Hal in *2001: A Space Odyssey*. If we could be fooled by Hal, what does that tell us about the role that our mental states may or may not play in determining our behavior? Maybe, like Hal's, our behavior is caused by sophisticated programming, and our impression that we are mentally in charge is an illusion. Buddhist meditators and experimenters with psychedelic drugs have described the realization that our minds are always a half-step behind our behavior, perpetually running to catch up.

MINDLESS CREATIVITY

If mental states don't *cause* anything, where do the mind's creations come from? Are all of our creations just outputs of our brain's hard-wiring? If so, shouldn't a sophisticated computer system be able to create a first-rate joke? You be the judge. Programmers gave this challenge to the supercomputers at Edinburgh University, and here is the kind of gag the machines generated:

"What kind of line has sixteen balls? A pool cue!"

Using a five-knee-slap scale, what do you think? Well, okay, then consider this one:

"What kind of murderer has moral fiber? A cereal killer."

Sure, it'd go over better in the middle-school cafeteria than on *Saturday Night Live*, but, hey, your brother-in-law has told worse, are we right?

As the mind-body debate has continued in our own day, it has gotten subtler and more complex, but its basic terms have not changed. There are still dualists of various stripes who claim that the mind is something different from the neuroelectrical impulses of the brain. And there are the physicalists who claim that mental states are identical to neural states. And then there are the functionalists, who are basically neutral on the issue, so who needs them?

ENTER ZOMBIES, LAUGHING

One entertaining philosophical contribution to the debate about what a mind might be is the so-called zombie problem. It seems particularly relevant to death, you know?

The zombie problem is a challenge to the physicalists, who say that after we describe the brain and how it works electrically, there's nothing left to describe. The workings of our "minds"—sensations, thoughts, intentions—are all subject to the laws of physics, and all our "changes of mind" are the result of physical, neuroelectrical causes.

The twentieth-century American philosopher Saul Kripke posed the ultimate physicalist question this way: Imagine a God who brings into existence a world that looks exactly like ours that operates purely by the laws of physics. Would the Creator have to do anything further to provide for human consciousness?

Ludwig Wittgenstein put it like this: "What is left over when I subtract the fact that my arm goes up from the fact that I raise my arm?"[4] (You may have to read that one twice. We did.)

Enter the zombists. Zombies, presumably, are human beings without consciousness, yet they move around and do all the things that other human beings do. So if zombies exist, that rules out physicalism, because if physicalism were true, the zombies would have consciousness!

ALL TOO HUMAN ZOMBIES

But wait one minute. Maybe zombies don't exist. (Personally, we've never seen one, and we've been to some really slow cocktail parties.) No problem, say the

The zombies were halfway across the living room
when they noticed that "Friends" was on.

trickier zombists. If it's even *possible* that zombies exist, that's good enough to challenge physicalism. So the zombists dream up *conceivable* scenarios. Says contemporary British philosopher Robert Kirk, we can conceive of micro-Lilliputians inside Gulliver's head who disconnect both his receptor nerves (input/perception) and his motor nerves (output/action). These little tricksters now receive all the inputs into Gulliver's brain and initiate their own signals to his muscles. Gulliver will seem to an observer to be just his ordinary self, but he will have no consciousness. He will be, in effect, a zombie. So, says Kirk, because we can conceive of this scenario, consciousness must be something different from just the physical inputs.

But wait, cry the physicalists! Being conceivable isn't the same thing as being possible! You can *conceive* of these nano-Lilliputians, but they're not really possible in the real world.

At this point the argument gets too wiggy for words, and our mind—or brain, you choose which—shuts down.

Wow! Finally something I get—philosophers have nothing better to do than to dream up little Disney characters.

Sure, but after they dream them up, they ask some pretty interesting questions about them.

Yeah, maybe interesting to a Disney character. Anyway, I

*think the soul is something different from the mind. Like it's
deeper. If I say somebody's soulful, I don't mean anything about
his mind. You know, like Aretha Franklin is the Queen of Soul,
not the Queen of Mind, and barbecued soul food is way more appealing than any "mind food." (I'm thinking ginkgo biloba
here.) And oh, one more thing—souls are good or bad morally. A
good mind is just sharp at plane geometry or gets straight As in
French, but someone with a good soul, that's a whole different
deal—that's a person who feels your pain. He's, like, in touch,
you know?*

Excellent points, Daryl. And the twentieth-century psychologist and philosopher of psychotherapy Otto Rank
agrees with you. He says the modern view that equates the
soul with the mind is way off the mark. He says that in primitive times "soul" meant "life-power." (Think James Brown
singing "I Feel Good.") And this life-power, or *mana*, was
everywhere and in everything.

In those good old primitive days when a man was a man,
and kids still helped out around the cave, death-anxiety had
not raised its scary head, because this universal life-power
was immortal. Not only was the Force with us, but we were
part of the Eternal Force. But soon the notion of life-power
got mixed together with the notion of individual *will*-power,
and once that happened, it was only a matter of time before
people realized that the will of some folks could break the will
of other folks. This could be life-threatening for the folks of
the second part—first of all literally, but secondly because the
primitive idea of will-power was so wrapped up with their

notion of life-power that any limit on their will-power brought on the heebie-jeebies of death-anxiety. In other words, the possibility of having their will crushed raised the threat of having their souls crushed in the process. Say goodbye to the happy innocent days of equal-access *mana*.

But even more powerful than the will of any individual was the will of the tribe, so people hooked up their individual wills to the will of their group and kin. This move had a fabulous extra benefit: because each individual was a part of the tribe, and the tribe was immortal, individuals could claim immortality.

According to Rank, around the biblical era, this collective will of the tribe got projected onto an even more transcendent entity—a monotheistic God—and that's when all hell broke loose. Now individual expressions of will were seen as rebellious, and ideas of sin and guilt developed. (One of the benefits of identifying with a group is that groups don't do guilt, or at least when they do, it gets nicely diluted.) With individual sin came the old death-anxiety blues again. Bad will = bad soul = bad life-power. "The wages of sin is death" is how Paul put it—just one reason why he was known around town as Pithy Paul.

Professor Rank was Jewish, but he thought Christian self-surrendering love was one cure for death-anxiety, because it beats death to the punch by dissolving the ego before death has a chance to do it. But Rank recognized that self-surrender is a stretch for most lovers, so he suggested looking to artists for clues; he believed artists were crucial to society's work of creating authentic responses to the anxiety of death. James Joyce undoubtedly ranked high on Rank's list of soulful artists.

So, does that sound more like what you had in mind by "soul," Daryl?

Well, yeah, I guess so. But I'm one of those guys who're not too good at self-surrendering love. Who is these days? And that artist cure doesn't do it for me. I know a lot about art, but I don't know what I like. What I want to know is if my soul, or will, or whatever, can live on forever. At this point in my life, I don't really care what happens to my body. I just want my "Me" to be immortal.

Okay, Daryl, you asked for it. So it's back to the golden days in Athens again.

Plato "proved" the immortality of the soul in several of his dialogues, but probably his best-known proof is in the dialogue "Meno," where Socrates demonstrates that the soul must have existed *before* a person was born.

Interestingly, most people aren't all that concerned with the possibility of eternal life *before* arriving on earth, possibly because even if they did exist then, they can't remember it. This sheds new light on the old question of what our post-earthly consciousness would be like if the soul were immortal. Would we be able to remember our earthly consciousness? If not, what's the big whoop about immortality? With no continuity of Me-ness, why should I care—either now or then? Or to put it another way, why should either of me care?

In any event, Socrates' proof of prenatal immortality is that one of Meno's uneducated slave boys actually comes up

with the Pythagorean theorem without ever having studied geometry! Therefore, he must be *remembering* it. You recall that theorem: in a right triangle, the square of the hypotenuse is equal to the sum of the squares of the other two sides. Huh? We can barely remember that from tenth grade, let alone from before we were born.

Socrates purports to only *guide* the boy into "discovering" the theorem that is lodged somewhere deep in his psyche. Here's Socrates at work, drawing with a stick on the ground:

> Soc.: Tell me, boy, do you know that a figure like this is a square?
> Boy: I do.
> Soc.: And you know that a square figure has these four lines equal?
> Boy: Certainly.
> Soc.: And these lines which I have drawn through the middle of the square are also equal?
> Boy: Yes.

And on Socrates goes, getting one-word answers from the boy, until the dénouement:

> Soc. (to Meno): Do you observe, Meno, that I am not teaching the boy anything, but only asking him questions; and now he fancies that he knows how long a line is necessary in order to produce a figure of eight square feet; does he not?[5]

To Socrates, this is proof that the boy is *recollecting* knowledge he already had, so *ipso facto,* an immortal psyche exists—in fact, an immortal psyche that got an A in plane geometry.

For a modern educator, the problem with the Meno proof is that it sure looks like Socrates is *teaching* the boy the theorem—using, well, the Socratic method of instructing via a series of Q&As.

Modern Meno

A husband and wife sign up for Chinese language lessons.

"Are you planning to go to China?" the instructor asks.

"Oh, no," says the man. "We just adopted a baby from China, and when he starts talking, we want to be able to understand what he's saying."

At the very least, Socrates' argument here raises questions about what memory actually is and how it works: *mysteriously,* it turns out.

Three elderly men visit a doctor for a memory test. The doctor asks the first one, "What's three times three?"

"285!" the man replies.

Worried, the doctor turns to the second man. "How about you? What's three times three?"

"Uh, Monday!" the second man shouts.

Even more concerned, the doctor motions to the third man.

"Well, what do you say? What's three times three?"

"Nine!" the third man replies.

"Excellent!" the doctor exclaims. "How did you get that?"

"Oh, easy," the man says. "You just subtract the 285 from Monday!"

In *The Republic*, Plato offers another dubious argument, this one "proving" the soul's indestructibility, but one question that he was unable to raise at the time is what has come to be known as the Eternal Fruitcake Conundrum, a case of an *inanimate* object that is indestructible. No lesser authorities than Dave Barry and Johnny Carson have weighed in on this puzzlement:

Barry: "Fruitcakes make ideal gifts because the Postal Service has been unable to find a way to damage them."

Carson: "There's actually only one fruitcake in the U.S., and it's passed around year after year from family to family."

So the question remains: Are fruitcakes immortal?

Feeling more immortal now, Daryl?
Are you kidding? I think this guy Plato's the fruitcake.

{ 8 }

Heaven—a Landscape to Die For

All right, you nerds, enough with the dead philosophers yapping from their graves! I don't know about you guys, but every night before I go to bed I pray to God I'll go to Heaven. You know, "If I should die before I wake" and like that. So give me the dope on Heaven, wouldya?

Okay, Daryl, we admit it: sometimes all this deep-think, edge-of-the-mind philosophy stuff seems so out of touch with what people actually believe, we feel like shouting at all those wackadoodle philosophers and theologians: "Get real!"

Fact is, in a comprehensive survey of Americans of every religious and nonreligious stripe, pollsters found that the great majority of us believe there is some sort of life after death, that everyone has a soul, and that Heaven and Hell are for real. (None of this, of course, would surprise Freud or Becker.)

A full 81 percent are confident in an afterlife of some kind, with only slightly fewer (79 percent) concurring with the statement "Every person has a soul that will live forever, either in God's presence or absence." What about Heaven? Seventy-six percent reported that they believe in Heaven, with some 5 percent fewer saying that they also believe in Hell.[1] (You gotta love that upbeat 5 percent.) As to what kind of heaven the majority has in mind, 60 percent of everyone surveyed described it as nothing more concrete than some kind of "state of eternal existence (with God)" or "merely symbolic," both of which sound alarmingly philosophical to us. Still, a full 30 percent of all Americans agreed with the statement that Heaven is "an *actual place* of rest and reward where souls go after death."

It's this "actual place" group that fires our imaginations. Although they represent a bit less than a third of the total population, these are the folks who set the stage for how the rest of us view Heaven—how it's decorated, how *you* look there, whom you're likely to meet, how you pass your (infinite) time, and who does the dishes.

KNOCK, KNOCK, KNOCKING HEAVEN

True believers in a literal Heaven take one hell of a beating in the Hollywood documentary *Heaven* (1987), directed by Diane Keaton. The film intersperses sermons by evangelicals, pontifications by bearded New Age prophets, and soliloquies by earnest regular folk with black-and-white archival clips of people falling in love and dancing on clouds in Hollywood Heaven. The film's winking attitude is "We know better."

For the record, most of Ms. Keaton's interviewees believe that Heaven is a city (one Bible scholar notes that the New Jerusalem is five thousand times the size of New York City), that its streets are either gold or crystal, and that there is an abundance of trees, chirping birds, and angels, along with all the people you ever loved and/or who loved you. One youngster states that Heaven is all white and mushy, like marshmallows, and in fact is convinced that one's diet there consists entirely of marshmallows.

Mansions, often made out of precious stones and minerals, figure prominently in the cityscape (one preacher stresses that they are rent-free with no fear of eviction). Most are certain that life in Heaven is pain-free, inhabitants never age, and they can eat fatty foods without fear of putting on weight. Interviewees were divided on the role of sex in Heaven, half thinking that residents are way beyond it, the other half thinking that orgasms in the Great Beyond are earth-shattering. There is general agreement that residents look exactly as they did in their earthly incarnation, although many also believe that there is no blood in their heavenly veins and that Up There, folks can walk through walls.

THE BIBLE SAYS IT'S SO, RIGHT?

The idea of Heaven as the final destination spot comes to us in all its glory from the Bible, right? Well, it depends on whom you ask.

Let's start with modern Bible scholars, and by "modern" we don't mean edgy hotshot geeks just out of graduate school; we mean mainstream Bible scholars of the last two hundred years or so. According to these folks, the primary meaning of "heaven" in the Hebrew Bible is simply "the firmament": the transparent dome between the waters above and the waters and earth below.[2]

The waters above? What's that—some kind of exclusive beach resort? Have I been missing something?

It's just the way those Old Testament types saw the cosmos, Daryl. They looked up into the sky and it looked kind of soupy up there in the Great Beyond. Remember, they didn't have telescopes yet.

To them, the firmament was where the sun, moon, stars, and birds, as well as God, hung out. But the main point is the ancient Hebrews had *no* concept of a life after death, let alone in the firmament. The very late prophet Daniel speaks of "everlasting life," with different outcomes for the righteous and the wicked, but it is framed in terms of resurrection—a return to life—rather than a continuation of life in some other place, like Beulah Land,[3] a.k.a. Paradise. So not even a glimmer of Heaven yet.

In the New Testament, most heaven references are to "the

kingdom of heaven," but the kingdom of heaven isn't Heaven. Okay, let's try that again. The kingdom of heaven is a euphemism for the kingdom of God, and the earliest Christians, who were originally Jewish, used that term because the name of God was considered too holy to utter.[4] The kingdom of heaven is not so much a place as a time—a future time "at the end of the age" when God's will prevails throughout the universe. That's why Christians pray, "Thy kingdom come, thy will be done." Jesus preached that this time was nigh, *very* nigh, and some passages sound as if he believed it was already here.

The modernists say that it was only after Jesus' death, when the disciples had profound spiritual experiences they interpreted as meaning Jesus was still alive, that a fully formed Christian notion of a general resurrection developed. Yet even in resurrection it is not the *individual* who "goes to Heaven" *at* death; it is "all the elect" who will be transformed at once—*at the end of history.* Likewise, Jesus' description of the fiery furnace "where there will be weeping and gnashing of teeth" refers, not to an afterlife Hell, but rather to the end of history, when the wicked will be excluded from the kingdom of God.

So, Daryl, the trip to Heaven (or Hell) when you die is one trip we don't think you should count on, although just in case, you may want to be prepared. Like Woody Allen, who said, **"I don't believe in an afterlife, although I am bringing a change of underwear."**

But if it's (literal) uplift you're looking for, check out the old-school Christian commentators on the Bible. They argue that there are plenty of passages in the Bible that point to a literal Heaven and/or Hell to which all of us will be assigned at the time of our death. For example, the Hebrew Bible speaks of Sheol, a sort of netherworld for departed spirits that roughly corresponds to Hades, although it is described more as a place of weariness than as a place of punishment.[5] The traditionalists also cite some Jesus quotables in the gospels that seem to refer to an immediate life-after-death in Heaven. For example, Luke depicts Jesus telling one of the criminals crucified with him, "*Today* you will be with me in Paradise."

That sounds like a very specific time and place and may allay Mr. Allen's fear that **"there is an afterlife, but no one will know where it's being held."**

Modern Bible scholars counter that while Jesus may have believed in a sort of temporary parking garage for the dead, he was way more interested in the coming reign of God and our having "eternal life" under his reign at the end of history than in any immediate afterlife in Heaven.

In any event, it is in the Book of Revelation that traditionalists find a gold mine of heavenly imagery. In the visions of John of Patmos, the wall of the New Jerusalem is made of jasper, and the city itself is pure as gold and clear as glass. The foundations are adorned with jewels, and lamps are unnecessary because God is the light of the city. It is also in the Book of Revelation that traditionalists find their picture of Hell, "a pool of fire and sulphur." Even though John specifically says these are visions of the Apocalypse at the end of history, old-school commentators like to attribute the imagery to an afterlife in Heaven or Hell. Modernists might suggest the conservatives check their source: John of P. was all alone on an island having, well, visions.

Interestingly enough, the traditionalists also pick up on Paul's description of the dawn of the new age at the end of history, even though it's hard to reconcile with the idea of an immediate Heaven. Paul says, "The dead in Christ will rise first. Then we who are alive, who are left, will be caught up in the clouds together with them to meet the Lord in the air; and so we will be with the Lord forever."[6] Dubbed "the Rapture" by conservative Christians, this event at the "Endtime" is the subject of the enormously popular "Left Behind" books by Tim LaHaye and Jerry B. Jenkins.

WWW.YOUVEBEENLEFTBEHIND.COM

A new website offers a service to those who anticipate being "taken up" in the Rapture and who are concerned about their friends and relatives left behind. For an annual fee (forty dollars for the first year), subscribers can post messages to be emailed to their loved ones six days after the Rapture. Members will be banking on there being at least a six-day window when their loved ones can still be persuaded to repent and accept Christ. "Our purpose is to get one last message to the lost, at a time when they might just be willing to hear it for the first and last time."

"I think that's enough peyote for one day."

What if the staff of www.youvebeenleftbehind.com have all been "taken up" in the Rapture? Who will be minding the store? Don't worry, they've got you covered. The system will go on alert automatically when three of the five staff members, scattered around the U.S., fail to log in over a three-day period. Presumably, the three-out-of-five rule is in case two of the five don't make the cut. And in case someone falsely triggers the system, there's another three-day waiting period before the emails are automatically sent.

Those Left-Behinders sure have all the exits covered.

ADMISSIONS POLICY

Not surprisingly, the great majority of people who believe Heaven exists also believe they are a shoo-in for being waved through the Pearly Gates. Forty-three percent are convinced they'll qualify because they have "confessed their sins and accepted Jesus Christ as their savior." Fifteen percent believe they have it knocked because "they have tried to obey the Ten Commandments," and another 15 percent because "they are basically a good person." Finally, a particularly sanguine group of 6 percent believe they will make it because "God loves all people and will not let them perish."

As for the admissions criteria in the Bible—whether admission to Heaven or eternal life—it all depends again

on whom you ask. In looking at the Hebrew Bible, conservatives tend to stress the Law: honor your father and mother; don't lose your cool around your neighbor's wife; eat borscht, don't eat mussels marinara. Liberals prefer the sweeping calls for justice in the books of the prophets. The prophets' exhortations aren't as specific as the Law, but some say they're even harder to live up to. They are summed up by the prophet Micah: "What does the Lord require of you but to do justice, and to love kindness, and to walk humbly with your God?"[7]

As for the New Testament, the old-schoolers emphasize Jesus' and Paul's more prescriptive sayings—for example, nix to divorce—while the liberals point to the fact that both Jesus and Paul seem to be way more interested in the spirit of the law than in its letter. For example, when a first-century lawyer wants to know the way to eternal life, Jesus tells him to love God with all his heart and soul and mind and strength, and to love his neighbor as himself.[8] No no-nos here.

To top it off, Jesus says elsewhere that we shouldn't be judging anybody else anyway. What? No prohibition of gay marriage? Don't you know anything about "Christian lifestyle," Jesus?

To understand the importance of the spirit vs. the letter of the law, check this woman out for attitude:

The police are called to an apartment, and when they get there, they find a dead body and a woman standing over it holding a bloody 5 iron. The detective says, "Lady, is that your husband?"

She says, "Yeah."

The detective says, "Did you hit him with that golf club?"

She says, "Yes, I did."

The detective says, "How many times did you hit him?"

She says, "I don't know . . . five, six, maybe seven times . . . just put me down for a five."

Although Paul sometimes tends to be a tough cookie, he tells us that eternal life is available as a gift, of all things. There's no way we can earn it! So much for admissions criteria.

Nonetheless, Christian denominations often talk as if there's a divine report card and only some of us make the dean's list. And many Christians believe that Saint Peter—the gatekeeper at the Pearly Gates—has been deputized to enforce the entrance policy and, like a doorman at a trendy club, engages the applicant in some edgy Q&A:

A man dies and goes to the Judgment. Saint Peter meets him at the Gates and says, "Before you meet with God, I thought I should tell you—we've looked at your life, and you really didn't do anything particularly good or bad. We're not sure what to do with you. Can you tell us anything you did that can help us make our decision?"

The applicant thinks a moment and replies, "Yeah, once I was driving along and came upon a woman who was being harassed by a group of bikers. So I pulled over, got out my tire iron, and went up to the leader of the bikers. He was a big, muscular, hairy guy with tattoos all over his body and a ring through his nose. Well, I tore out his nose ring and told him he and his gang had better stop bothering the woman or they would have to deal with me!"

"I'm impressed," Saint Peter responds. "When did this happen?"

"About two minutes ago."

As it turns out, Saint Peter's in-depth interview technique yields critical admissions data:

It got crowded in Heaven, so Saint Peter decided to accept only people who'd had a really bad day on the day they died. On the first morning of the new policy, Saint Peter said to the first man in line, "Tell me about the day you died."

The man said, "Oh, it was awful. I was sure my wife was having an affair, so I came home early from work to catch her in the act. I searched all over the apartment and couldn't find her lover anywhere. So finally I went out on the balcony, where I found this man hanging over the edge by his fingertips. So I went inside, got a hammer, and started hitting his hands. He fell, but landed in some bushes and survived. So I went inside, picked up the refrigerator, and pushed it out over the balcony. It crushed him, but the strain of hefting the fridge gave me a heart attack and I died."

Saint Peter couldn't deny this was an awful day and that it was a crime of passion, so he let the man enter Heaven. He then asked the next man in line about the day he died.

"Well, sir, it was terrible. I was doing aerobics on the balcony of my apartment when I slipped over the edge. I managed to grab the balcony of the apartment below me but then some maniac came out and started pounding my fingers with a hammer! I fell, but I landed in some bushes and lived! But then this guy came out again and dropped a refrigerator on me! That did it!"

Saint Peter chuckled a bit, and let him into Heaven. "Tell me about the day you died," he said to the third man.

"Okay, picture this. I'm naked, hiding in a refrigerator . . ."

NE'ER THE TWAIN SHALL MEET
Heaven goes by favor. If it went by merit, you would stay out and your dog would go in.

—Mark Twain

Concepts of Heaven and Hell are determined not only by religious sect, but also by secular culture.

Take the case of André, a resident of Heaven, who asked to visit his old friend, Pierre, in Hell. His wish was granted, and Satan himself led André to his friend's private suite.

There Pierre was, seated in a loveseat with a gorgeous naked woman on his lap, a tray of hors d'oeuvres on the table next to him, and a champagne flute in his hand. André couldn't believe his eyes. "This is Hell?" he exclaimed.

"But yes," Pierre sighed. "The woman, she is my first wife. The cheese is from Belgium. And this 'champagne'—what can I say?—it is not even real, it's from California!"

Hey, you say, where does the picture of Saint Peter at the Pearly Gates come from? In the Gospel of Matthew, Jesus says he is giving Peter the "keys of the *kingdom of heaven.*" He apparently means that Peter has a central role in ushering in the new era, which may seem a little vaguer than list-checking at the entrance to a gated community, but that's where we get St. Pete *qua* doorman. In the Book of Revelation, one of the details of John's visions of the New Jerusalem is that it had twelve gates and each gate "was a single pearl." Put it all together and whaddya got? Saint Peter at the pearly gates.

YOUR HEAVEN OR MINE?

One criterion to bear in mind when choosing a religion is where its particular afterlife is being held. Consider Pure Land Buddhism. Based on the belief that in our degenerate Age of Dharma Decline it is too difficult for most of us to reach the void of Nirvana through meditation alone, Pure Land Buddhism offers visions of celestial Buddha lands we can reach by devotion to Amitabha Buddha. At the end of life, when we pass over to these exquisite lands, we will find it much easier to attain Nirvana there.

In the "Sutra of Visualization" the Buddha tells us how to attain a vision of the Buddha lands. In a trance, we can visualize the giant trees adorned with blossoms and leaves made of seven kinds of jewels. Those made of lapis lazuli emit a golden light; the rock crystal blossoms, a crimson light; the emerald-colored leaves, a sapphire light; the sapphire-colored leaves, a pearl-green light. It's like being sentenced to prism. Nets of pearls cover the trees. Between the nets are five billion flower palaces, and within each flower palace are celestial children who wear ornaments of the five billion wish-fulfilling jewels. (Steven Spielberg couldn't do it justice. "We ran the five billion flower palaces by Production, Steve. Sorry, you're going to have to live with thirty flower palaces.")

Muslim Paradise is equally exotic. According to the Koran, those who reach it will "recline on jeweled couches face to face, and there shall wait on them immortal youths with bowls and ewers and a cup of purest wine (that will neither pain their heads nor take away their reason); with fruits of their own choice and flesh of fowls that they relish. And theirs shall be the dark-eyed nymphs, chaste as hidden pearls: a reward for their deeds. . . . We created the nymphs and made them virgins, loving companions for those on the right hand. . . ."9

The famous seventy-two virgins are not mentioned in the Koran, and their provenance is long and very complicated. According to one compilation of *hadith* (Islamic traditions), the story was told by one man who got it from another man who got it from a third man who heard Muhammad say, "The smallest reward for the people of Heaven is an abode where there are eighty thousand servants and seventy-two virgins."[10] Muslim clerics call this chain of transmission "weak," so we wouldn't bet the farm on there being exactly seventy-two, Daryl. Besides, maybe it's because we're on Social Security, but seventy-two virgins seems a bit excessive to us. Now the eighty thousand servants, that's a different matter.

Unsurprisingly, the vision of Heaven passed down by a religious tradition often turns out to reflect the general spirit of that tradition. In Hinduism, for example, none of the many layers of their multitiered Heaven is "Paradise." The many tiers are only increasingly refined levels of purgatory we pass through as determined by our karma—on our way to the real goal, the transcendence of *all* existence.

Confucius, by contrast, refused to speculate about Heaven altogether, though he accepted it as the abode of the venerable ancestors. Otherwise, he thought Heaven was a distraction from his practical ethic of right relationships.

But our favorite vision of a Heaven that reflects the spirit of its religious tradition is the Norse mythology surrounding Valhalla, the palace of slain warriors, where the roof is made of gold shields. The departed warriors feast every day on the flesh of a wild boar and drink liquor from the teat of a goat. Their principal pastime is clobbering each other. Kind of like celestial Ultimate Fighting.

WALL-TO-WALL CLOUDS
VS. WALL-TO-WALL GREENERY

Thank heaven for artists. Or to put it another way, thank artists for Heaven. It was the guys in smocks who gave us the Heaven we know—the one replete with terrific production values.

Much of our current imagery of Heaven came to us by way of late Middle Ages and Renaissance paintings. Consider an early-sixteenth-century painting, *The Holy Trinity Enthroned*, by an artist who is known only by his patron name, Master of James IV of Scotland (MJ4 to his rapper friends). Here we see some of Heaven's enduring hallmarks. Heaven is suspended in the sky above the clouds, which means it's *up*, a direction that depends on where on the globe you're standing (unless you happen to be a Flat Earthist). Clouds have always figured prominently in many concepts of Heaven: sometimes we're high above them, but most often they're the wispy ground we walk upon. Furthermore, the furnishings, such as they are, are depicted in this painting in muted, super-pastel tones. Primary colors are definitely too garish for Heaven. And finally, for just a touch more color, we see hints of rainbows floating around MJ4's Divines. There appear to be no rainy days in Heaven, but rainbows aplenty.

Or take a look at *The Burial of the Count of Orgaz* from the Greek-born late-sixteenth-century painter Doménikos Theotokópoulos. (In his adopted home of Spain he opted for the nickname El Greco, because he thought it was easier to spell.) We see that not only has the paleness of Heaven faded to near-transparent whiteness, but two more of Heaven's persisting features appear: wardrobe-wise, togas or white choir robes are definitely in. (Heaven is an equal-opportunity community—universal togas and choir robes, like school uniforms, keep the rich from lording it over the riffraff.) Halos and wings appear to be optional for the *hoi polloi*. Finally, the airspace is heavily populated with gravity-defying adorables, cherubs and winged angels. As these darlings multiply in paintings throughout the Renaissance, golden lyres and harps become accessories *de la mode*. Along with the harps, here and there we start to see depictions of the heavenly choir, or at least of the soprano section.

Many art historians consider depictions of the Garden of Eden—i.e., heaven on earth—as a clue to the landscape of Heaven. It's Heaven once removed, but nonetheless easier to wrap our earthbound senses around. Take the Garden as rendered by fifteenth-century Nederlandish painter Hieronymus Bosch. (Born Jeroen Anthonissen van Aken, he changed his name because he thought Hieronymus was harder to spell.) In the left-hand panel of his famous triptych *The Garden of Earthly Delights,* a panel that is alternately called "Paradise" or "The Garden of Eden," H.B. contributes some topical features of this version of Heaven: it's rural, lush, and teeming with lovable, people-friendly critters—the Peaceable Kingdom with lots of low-hanging, fiber-rich fruit. Reminds us of a story:

Al and Betty were eighty-three years old and had been married for sixty years. Though far from rich, they managed to get by through watching their pennies. They were both in very good health, largely due to Betty's insistence on a healthful diet.

On their way to their sixty-fifth high school reunion their plane crashed, sending them off to Heaven. At the Pearly Gates Saint Peter escorted them to a beautiful mansion furnished in gold and fine silks, with a fully stocked kitchen and a waterfall in the master bath. A maid could be seen hanging their favorite clothes in the closet. They gasped in astonishment when Saint Peter said, "Welcome to Heaven. This will be your home now. It is your reward."

Al looked out the window and saw a championship golf course, more beautiful than any he had ever seen. Saint Peter led them to the clubhouse, where they saw the lavish buffet lunch, with every imaginable delicacy laid out before them, from lobster thermidor to filet mignon to creamy desserts. Al glanced nervously at Betty, then turned to their host. "Where are the low-fat and low-cholesterol foods?" he asked.

"That's the best part," Saint Peter replied. "You can eat as much as you like of whatever you like, and you will never get fat or sick. This is Heaven!"

"No testing my blood sugar or blood pressure?" Al persisted.

"Never again," said St. Pete. "All you do here is enjoy yourself."

Al glared at Betty and groaned, "You and your stupid oat bran! We could have been here ten years ago!"

Starting with these basics, Bible illustrations, magazine ads, children's books, cartoons, and films filled in much of the rest of Heaven's imagery.

HEAVEN FOR BEGINNERS

Children's books that describe Heaven continue to proliferate faster than, say, micro-breweries. Recently, Maria Shriver (a.k.a. Mrs. Terminator) came out with *What's Heaven?*, a Q&A between a mother and daughter after the little girl's grandmother dies. When the girl asks why she can't see Heaven, Mom replies with philosophical sophistication, "Heaven isn't a place you can see. It's somewhere you believe in."

But our favorite Heaven in a kids' book is Cynthia Rylant's *Dog Heaven*. Dead doggies don't need wings because they'd rather run, and God, pictured as an old farmer with a white mustache and a goofy hat, wants doggies to do what comes naturally. This Heaven is decidedly Eden-like, filled with lakes and geese and angel children to play with. Most importantly, if you are a dog, Heaven is filled with artisanal dog biscuits shaped like kitty-cats, squirrels, and ham sandwiches. Woof!

Judging by Bible illustrations, Heaven's denizens are perpetually contented-looking to a point just short of smug. They tend to gather and lounge in small groups, favoring the shade of feathery-leafed trees. God himself, often accompanied by an entourage of saints, makes occasional appearances.

*"You faked your death once before—
how do I know you're not faking it now?"*

"I guess this is as good as it gets."

He wears a toga like everyone else, but his is, well, more flowy, not that anyone is complaining.

Heaven is one of the most popular locales for cartoons, right up there with desert islands and psychiatrists' offices. In most of them, the action takes place at the Pearly Gates with gags about entrance policies.

(Incidentally, cartoonists heavily favor "cloud" Heaven over "mountain greenery" Heaven, possibly because they usually work in black-and-white.)

Once inside the gates, we get a droll comedy of manners: here we are in the Great Beyond, but we're still basically human with all our earthly foibles, neuroses, and banality.

Not to be a downer, but the cartoon of card-playing Heaven has brought up a perennial worry of ours: Is eternity—even in Heaven—likely to bring on that old *ennui*? Consider Gil, an inveterate fisherman.

Gil is casting his line along a beautiful stream when he snags a gorgeous twenty-pound salmon. But just as he is hauling it in, he has a massive heart attack.

When he comes to consciousness, he sees that he is lying beside an even more beautiful stream and that it is teeming with salmon. Next to him is a state-of-the-art rod and reel. He grabs it and casts his line. Bingo! Gil immediately catches a spectacular thirty-five-pound salmon and reels it in. He feels terrific. He casts again, and once again he instantly snags a fantastic fish. On and on he goes, the glorious fish lying in a long row on the bank behind him.

But as the afternoon wears on, Gil realizes that he is no longer fishing with his usual enthusiasm. In fact, he's starting to feel bored.

Just then, he sees another man walking along the stream bank toward him. "So, this is Heaven," Gil calls to the other man.

"You think so?" comes the reply.

HEAVEN FOR REEL

It was the Hereafter via the movies that gave Heaven its juiciest details. Consider the silent 1926 black-and-white German classic *Faust*. Although the film doesn't focus on day-to-day Heaven, its image of Faust sailing through the space-time continuum with the devil at his side offers a glimpse of Heaven's landscape: bright rays of light piercing the mist and classical Greek edifices apparently abandoned before they were completely built. Much of the imagery is derived from sourpuss artists like Dürer and Bruegel, so *Faust*'s Heaven looks murky and mysterious as hell, not a real happy place to spend eternity.

Mist became a must in later films. In the 1941 comedy *Here Comes Mr. Jordan,* we see what became known in Hollywood special effects departments as "dry ice" Heaven—wall-to-wall wispy, smoky, cloudy stuff the departed can walk on.

Heaven plays no more than a walk-on role in the 1943 all-black movie musical *Cabin in the Sky,* but it's worth noting that they're still walking on clouds there. And in keeping with the script's period stereotypes of childlike, poor-but-perpetually-happy African-Americans, their stairway to Heaven is made of rickety, falling-apart two-by-fours, not that anybody minds.

Only a few years after *Jordan* and *Cabin* came a surprisingly sophisticated Heaven in the British film *A Matter of Life and Death* (retitled *Stairway to Heaven* for American release). Visually, its most witty conceit is that Heaven is in black-and-white, while life on earth is in vivid color. (A Heaven-dweller down on earth for some business remarks, "One is *starved* for Technicolor up there.") This Heaven is terribly austere and all business; keeping records of who died exactly when keeps clerks busy all day. The look is 1940s futuristic—conveyor belts of the recently deceased, pairs of wings on department store garment racks, an automatic soda machine.

The plot of *A Matter of Life and Death* is strictly "high concept," but it raises some good old-fashioned philosophical questions: Is heaven only a hallucination, the result of brain damage that can be fixed by surgery? Is one's willingness to die for a loved one the ultimate litmus test for true love? Is it better to live in black-and-white than in Technicolor?

This last question suggests that Heaven is itself a movie, or at least a good set on which to make one.

When the great Hollywood producer-director Otto Preminger arrived in heaven, Saint Peter met him at the Pearly Gates and explained that God would like the director to make one more movie.

Preminger grimaced. "But I retired years before I died. I'm tired of all the hassles involved in making movies."

"Listen," Saint Peter explained, "we got Ludwig van Beethoven to write a new score for the movie ..."

"You're not listening to me," Preminger protested. "I don't want to make any more movies."

"But we've got Leonardo da Vinci to do the set design for you," Saint Peter exclaimed.

"I don't want to make any more movies!" the director insisted.

"Just look at this script," Saint Peter said. "We got William Shakespeare to write it for you!"

"Well," said Preminger, "a score by Beethoven, set design by Leonardo, a script by Shakespeare ... How can I go wrong? I'll do it!"

"Great!" exclaimed Saint Peter. "There's just one small favor ... I've got this girlfriend who sings ..."

Kitsch heaven goes over the top in the 1998 extravaganza *What Dreams May Come*. This was the first Hollywood Heaven flick to take full advantage of the post–*Star Wars* special effects revolution, so obviously the filmmakers went the Garden of Eden route—it's a Monet landscape peppered with Kmart art, then digitalized with flying dogs, fairies, and hot babes. What we get here is Sensory Overload Heaven: every view is crowded with calendar images of beams of golden light, rainbows, cloud-encircled mountains, gurgling streams, blossoming trees, and wildflowers, not to mention Greco-Roman dwellings replete with classical columns and 1950s lawn furniture. It's heaven for people with ADD.

No surprise that when it comes to philosophical questions, *What Dreams May Come* is strictly of the New Age Airhead school of deep-think. An archangel intones, "You create your own image of heaven from your imagination," "Thought is real, physical is the illusion," and "Here is big enough for everyone to have his own private universe." *How's that again?* It's enough to make a Zen master giggle.

Thankfully, Monty Python's *The Meaning of Life—Part VII: Death* gives us a wacky Heaven that is more lively and joyful than all the rest—even if it is Satirical Heaven.

But before Monty's Flying Circus takes us there, we can't resist sharing their hilarious setup. The Grim Reaper comes knocking on the door of the country home of some British bourgeoisie where a dinner party is in progress. The host, in blazer and tie, opens up and sees G.R. with his scythe. "Is it about the hedge?" he asks. The wife arrives and invites the Reaper in, simpering to the guests, "It's one of the men from the village," and then, "Do get Mr. Death a drink, dear."

Unamused, G.R. informs them, "I have come to take you away." To which one of the guests replies, "Well, that's cast rather a gloom over the evening, hasn't it?"

Zippity-zip and they are *all* (the salmon loaf the hostess served happened to be laced with botulism) off to Heaven, arriving at the check-in counter of a modern hotel done up in shades of white. From there the guests are directed to the Red Room, a Las Vegasy theater, the tables crowded with cheerful types from various eras. And suddenly the show begins: a music and dance extravaganza starring a Tom Jones look-alike and featuring angels-cum-chorus-girls with their heavenly breasts exposed. (The popular cartoon feature *South Park: Bigger, Longer & Uncut* also featured bare-chested, bosomy angels—are we spotting a trend here?)

The Meaning of Life ends with a woman by a hearth saying that the meaning of life is, well, uh, and then the usual platitudes: be nice to one another, eat well, enjoy the ride. In context, it is strangely reassuring.

THE HELL, WE SAY

Don't get us started on Hell, the afterlife destination for sinners. Like Heaven, Hell has a post-biblical life of its own, its fiery decor fleshed out by painters, illustrators, cartoonists, and filmmakers, not to mention poets like Dante, whose Inferno gives us nine different levels of helldom. Some of our imagery of this netherworld comes to us via Greek mythology's Hades, a tough neighborhood on the other side of the River Styx, but most of it comes out of artists' and comedians' nightmares.

Suffice it to say that Hell adds one more reason to be angst-filled about death *even if there is an afterlife:* What if our souls *are* eternal but they end up in this torture chamber?

Let's not go there.

As usual, the country singers seem to be more down-to-earth than the painters and moviemakers. As Loretta Lynn sings it:

Everybody wants to go to heaven, but nobody wants to die.
Lord, I wanna go to heaven, but I don't wanna die.
Well, I long for the day when I'll have new birth, 'cause I
    love the livin' here on earth.
Everybody wants to go to heaven, but nobody wants to die.

Tell it like it is, Loretta!
We're with you, Daryl. Pass the oat bran!

· IV ·

Post Mortem Life:
Postcards from
the Other Side

✦

Is that your late Aunt Lulu on the phone?
If so, is it bad manners to hang up?

9

Tunnel Vision

Okay, Daryl, you know the drill: Your heart stops, your lungs cease pumping, your vital signs sign off . . . and suddenly you lift off from your body and hover overhead—in fact, you hover over your own discarded body! And you feel terrific, beatific, like a million bucks. You know you're dead, but it's not a downer—it's an upper! That's when the music fades in—a celestial serenade, harps, choirs, maybe a flute or two. Gorgeous.

Hey, what's that brilliant swirl of light in the distance? You are ineluctably drawn toward it. It's at the end of a long tunnel. Gotta go there, just gotta. But wait, who's that standing at the entrance? Uncle Bertie? "Hey, Daryl, wassup?" "Unc, I haven't seen you since . . . omigosh . . . since you died in 1987! Wow!" And Aunt Lulu. My old soccer coach, Billy Wasalinski. Frank Sinatra . . .

Holy Moses! This is it! I'm on my way to Heaven!

Suddenly, a sepia-toned film starts playing in front of you. It's your very own biopic, the events—or at least the highlights—of your life on earth unfolding on the screen. Look, there's your old doggie, Buster, racing across the grass toward you when you were only six!

But just then a voice booms from above.

"Not so fast, Daryl," the voice says. "Your time has not yet come. You still have unfinished business on this side. You have to go back and complete your term as treasurer of the Knights of Columbus."

And that's when you wake up on the operating table, gasping for breath. "Wha . . . What hap—happened?" you manage to sputter.

A woman in a white coat looms over you. "You were gone for a bit there, Daryl," she says.

"Gone?"

"Clinically dead," she says, pointing to a heart monitor.

"For how long?"

"Oh, about ten seconds," she replies.

That's when you realize that you have just had a near-death experience, a phenomenon so popular that it is known to the in-crowd as simply NDE.

You are in great company, Daryl. The list of glitterati who've had NDEs includes Elizabeth Taylor, Sharon Stone, Peter Sellers, Gary Busey, Erik Estrada, Donald Sutherland, Burt Reynolds, Chevy Chase, and Ozzy Osbourne, who actually "died" twice after a bike accident that left him in a coma for eight days. Just so you know we aren't talking about run-of-the-mill kooks here.

The NDE craze took off with the 1975 publication of *Life After Life: The Investigation of a Phenomenon—Survival of Bodily Death* by Raymond Moody. Hundreds of unrelated people interviewed by Moody reported all or at least some of the experiences that you, Daryl, just had. The book was a huge bestseller. A film based on it hit the theaters. More and more NDEs were reported and, with the advent of the Net, NDEers got in touch with one another to compare experiences.

NDEs appeared to prove not only that there is an afterlife after all, but that the whole religion package is based on genuine experiences. What we had here was no less than *empirical evidence* of Heaven, Hell, God, Satan, telepathy, and doggie angels.

But wouldn't you know it, just when the NDEers thought they had their case locked, along came some science and philosophy types to do their usual killjoy thing. These skeptics usually start off by admitting that they cannot *dis*prove the existence of an afterlife, or even of a foretaste of it during "clinical death," but on the other hand, the evidence offered—subjective reports of NDEs—does not prove the existence of an afterlife either. As with any paranormal experience—say, seeing flying teapots circling your wife's head—there is no objective test to validate the person's experience. The principal question with NDEs is whether the experience has any connection to our "regular" empirical reality (the "real world"), as opposed to, say, being caused by brain farts.

"Last week, I think I had a near-life experience."

Sudden snaps in the synapses are the skeptics' alternative explanation for the near-death experiences—they are an unusual form of brain activity, probably kicked into action by the trauma of kicking the bucket. Neurosurgeon Philip Carter reports, "The brain is the ultimate computer. When it shuts down and reboots, it comes back with a lot of activity that can cause changes." He suggests that both the experience and the memory of the NDE are the product of a brain altered by the event, just as epileptics who report memories of transcendental experiences during seizures have had unusual brain events that can be recorded by an EEG.

The monitor confirmed cardiac arrest as an elderly man suddenly lost consciousness. After about twenty seconds of resuscitation, he came to. Explaining to him that his heart had momentarily stopped, the doctor asked if he remembered anything unusual during that time.

"I saw a bright light," he said, "and in front of me a man dressed in white."

Excitedly, the doctor asked if he could describe the figure.

"Sure, Doc," he replied. "It was you."

When NDEers argue back that a huge number of people report having similar near-death experiences and that this constitutes some kind of inter-subjective consensus, the skeptics remain skeptical, pointing out that the similarity of details in NDEs is undoubtedly the product of communication—just about everyone knows what an NDE *should* be like from watching TV, or from reading Moody's book, for that matter. They may also cite the fact that over 20 percent of Americans believe they have experienced alien abduction—not to mention a little inter-life-form hanky-panky. This stat casts a certain doubt over the NDE inter-subjectivity argument.

Carter and others actually think these NDEs are terrific—not because they signal an afterlife, but because they suggest the process of dying can be a pleasant one. Still, they find that only about 10 percent of near-deathers actually have one of these pleasant experiences; the great majority just feel scared and awful as they conk out.

But hang in there a minute, Daryl. There are also philosophers (not to mention mystics galore) who hold that altered mental states, whatever their origin—like, say, from ingesting a "magic mushroom"—give us a different kind of information, information about a "reality" that exists outside the boundaries of time and space. The nineteenth-century American philosopher William James certainly thought so. In his masterwork, *The Varieties of Religious Experience,* James writes about his experiences under the influence of the drug nitrous oxide:

> One conclusion was forced upon my mind at that time, and my impression of its truth has ever since remained unshaken. It is that our normal waking consciousness, rational consciousness as we call it, is but *one* special type of consciousness, whilst all about it, parted from it by the flimsiest of screens,

there lie potential forms of consciousness entirely different. We may go through life without suspecting their existence; but apply the requisite stimulus, and at a touch they are there in all their completeness, definite types of mentality which probably somewhere have their field of application and adaptation.[1]

If James's POV sounds familiar, that's probably because it resonates with the observations that Jill Bolte Taylor made while observing herself have a stroke. Or maybe it's because you frequent the same pub we do, the one with a sign behind the bar that says, **"Reality is a hallucination brought on by lack of alcohol."**

10

The Original Knock-Knock Joke

So while you guys are buried in your books trying to figure out if there's an immortal soul, my Gladys is chatting with her great-aunt Edna every night.

What's that got to do with anything?

Aunt Edna has been dead for thirty years.

Ah, yes, the so-called séance. Actually, Daryl, there are some bona fide philosophers—men like William James and the nineteenth-century British ethicist Henry Sidgwick—who snuck off into darkened rooms for the very same reason. Not to talk to Edna, of course, but to others on the Other Side.

And the overwhelming response of the rest of the academic and scientific community was, "Have these good men vacated their gourds?"

But in the 1870s, weirdness was in the air. Madame Blavatsky, a flamboyant Russian American by way of Tibet, founded the Theosophical Society in New York in 1875, dedicated to the study of "spiritualism." Séances were the rage in both England and America. A popular song of the day, "Spirit Rappings," was at once a harbinger of the New Age movement and arguably the first rap hit:

> Softly, softly, hear the rustle
> Of the Spirits' airy wings;
> They are coming down to mingle
> Once again with earthly things. . . .
> Rap-tap-tap lost friends are near you;
> Rap-tap-tap they see and hear you. . . .

Rap-tap-tap? What could the renowned Harvard professor, Mr. James, possibly have had on his mind?

As it happens, James (brother of Henry, no relation to Jesse), had *open-mindedness* on his mind. His American-style theory of knowledge maintained that truth is not static; rather, it is constantly evolving. And the *materialists*—philosophers ranging from Lucretius to Thomas Hobbes who believed that *only* the material world is real—were trying to stop truth in its tracks. For James, true theories are *useful* theories; not only do they square with all the known facts, they open the way to discovering future truths. If the future turns out to contradict today's truths, no problem: we'll own up to these contradictions and declare those theories false. But in the meantime, if a hypothesis guides our actions satisfactorily, then it is true enough for James to call it, well, "Truth." (Unfortunately, Stephen Colbert was not around yet to supply James with his neologism, "truthiness.")

According to James's epistemology, denying out of hand the possibility of a spirit's surviving the body was *dogmatic* materialism: it slammed the door closed on the possibility of newly revealed truth.

Tap, tap, rap, rap, open your minds to new possibilities, academic bigwigs!

What's more, James defended the "will to believe," specifically when it came to religion. By that he meant our "right to believe anything that is live enough to tempt our will." While we do not have the right to believe anything that is incompatible with the facts as we know them, when it comes to matters of religious belief or belief in free will—*where the known facts are insufficient to decide the question*—we are free to choose the way that seems best to us. James wittily showed how this operated when he wrote in his diary, "My first act of free will shall be to believe in free will."

INDELIBLE MARX

James thought a useful way to divide philosophers was "tough-minded" versus "tender-minded." The tender-minded are more interested in principles than in facts, more interested in ideas than in sensory evidence, more idealistic, optimistic, religious, and inclined to believe in free will. The tough-minded are more interested in hard facts than in principles, more trusting in sensory evidence than in ideas, more materialistic, pessimistic, irreligious, fatalistic, and skeptical. Each feels superior to the other: the tough think the tender are sentimental muttonheads; the tender think the tough are unrefined and callous. Most of us, James believed, are a mixture of the two. But clearly, James had not met Groucho Marx. (Actually, there's a pretty good reason for that.)

Groucho, if whimsical, was *thoroughly* tough-minded. He once reluctantly consented to join a group of friends visiting a popular and very expensive Hollywood medium. The spiritualist went around the table summoning up dead relatives, relaying messages from them, making predictions, and confidently answering all questions. After two hours, the spiritualist said, "My medium angel is getting tired. I have time for only one more question. You can find out anything you want."

Chimed Groucho, "What's the capital of North Dakota?"

But back to the nineteenth century, when the Society for Psychical Research in England and its American affiliate, the American Society for Psychical Research (both of which still exist), approached the subject of the spirit world with fear and trembling—not because they were afraid of ghosts, but because the academic reputations of their members were at stake. They clearly saw it was in their own best interest to be as skeptical as possible of every claim of every medium.

Sure enough, *tippity-tap*, Madame Blavatsky was exposed as a fraud, despite the fact that she had long resisted investigation by the Societies by claiming that her work was best carried out in a gilded shrine she had built in Madras, India. That shrine allegedly included tiny drawers in which "spirit letters" from the dead would suddenly appear. But Richard Hodgson, an Australian philosophy student of James's British colleague, Henry Sidgwick, gained access to the shrine and discovered double-sided drawers through which Mme. Blavatsky's servants were passing the letters. Seems Madame B. was counterfeiting missives from the deceased by finding letters they had written while still on "this side," steaming them open, thereby garnering personal information, resealing them, then imitating the handwriting of the dear departed to create the "spirit letters" full of private info. Thus did Madame Blavatsky anticipate communications theorist Marshall McLuhan's immortal words, "The medium is the message."

SCIENCE, SÉANCE, AS LONG AS YOU'RE HEALTHY

A ventriloquist goes to see his agent, desperate for work. And the agent says he's so sorry, but there isn't much demand for his act anymore, what with live variety shows gone, Ed Sullivan gone. About the only advice he has is the same he gave to another ventriloquist client—open a séance business.

So the ventriloquist thinks about it, finally finds a storefront for a good price, and puts up his shingle. The first customer who walks in is a bereaved widow. She wants to talk to her recently departed husband. "How much does it cost?"

The ventriloquist says: "Well, for $50, you can ask him any question you want, and he'll reply 'Yes' or 'No' with one knock on the table or two knocks, respectively. For $150, you can ask him any question you want, and he will answer you verbally. And then there's my $500 special."

The woman asks, "What's that?"

The ventriloquist says, "Well, you can ask him any question you want, he'll answer you verbally, and all the while I'll be drinking a glass of water."

THE RIGHTS OF THE DEPARTED

Lost in discussions of séances is any consideration for the dead respondents. Why do they have to appear on demand? Might they not have busy schedules too? Aren't they at least entitled to caller ID?

The longtime waiter was mourned by his customers after he passed away. So beloved was he that several patrons organized a séance in the restaurant to try to contact him.

They all held hands in the dark around the table as the medium called out: "Snark Withers! I summon the spirit of Snark Withers!"

Silence.

"Snark Withers!" the medium called out again. "I summon the spirit of Snark Withers!"

Once again, silence. The people around the table grew restless. Sensing a problem, the medium bellowed, "I command the spirit of Snark Withers to come forward!"

And sure enough, an apparition appeared floating above the table, and all recognized the image of their lost friend.

"Great to see you!" said one of the patrons. "But why did it take so long for you to come?"

Turning up his nose in disgust, the ghost replied, "This isn't my table!"

Yet both Sidgwick and James continued to hold open the possibility that among all the frauds there might be some genuine mediums with a genuine power to contact the dead—5 percent, they speculated. (Don't ask.) One medium they considered very promising was Eusapia Palladino, an Italian who would become sexually aroused when she entered the trance state and curl up on the laps of male participants. (Thus the expression, "The medium is the *massage*.")

But sure enough, German-American psychologist Hugo

Munsterberg caught Eusapia cheating: she wriggled out of her shoe, which was resting on his foot, and with her bare foot moved a small table behind her. James was furious at Munsterberg. Yes, Eusapia had cheated here and there, but that still didn't explain all of the parapsychological phenomena that occurred when she was closely monitored. Apparently, Eusapia brought out James's tender-mindedness. It was that lap thing that did it.[1]

HOW WOULD WILLIAM JAMES CALL THIS ONE?

For months, Mrs. Pitzel had been nagging her husband to go with her to the séance parlor of Madame Freda. "Milty, she's a real gypsy, and she brings the voices of the dead from the other world. We all talk to them! Last week I talked with my mother, may she rest in peace. Milty, for twenty dollars you can talk to your grampy whom you miss so much!"

Milton Pitzel could not resist her appeal. At the very next séance at Madame Freda's Séance Parlor, Milty sat under the colored light at the green table, holding hands with the person on each side. All were humming, "Oooom, oooom, tonka tooom."

Madame Freda, her eyes lost in trance, was making passes over a crystal ball. "My medium... Vashtri," she called. "Come in. Who is that with you? Who? Mr. Pitzel? Milton Pitzel's grandfather?"

Milty swallowed the lump in his throat and called, "Grampy?"

"Ah, Milteleh?" a thin voice quavered.

"Yes! Yes!" cried Milty. "This is your Milty! Grampy—*zayde*—are you happy in the other world?"

"Milteleh, I am in bliss. With your bubbie together, we laugh, we sing. We gaze upon the shining face of the Lord!"

A dozen more questions did Milty ask of his zayde, and each question did his zayde answer, until, "So now, Milteleh, I have to go. The angels are calling. Just one more question I can answer. Ask. Ask."

"Zayde," sighed Milty, "so when did you learn to speak English?"

REFLECTING ON THE DEAD

Leave it to the New Agers to channel the rap-tap-tap movement into a popular twenty-first-century consumer item, the *psychomanteum*. This is a dimly lit room where, for a fee, one can gaze into a large mirror, fall into a trance, and commune with the dead. *Psychomantea* date back to the ancient Greeks, who would gaze into reflecting pools to summon up the spirit world.

Some modern psychologists insist that the whole deal is just a hallucination resulting from a form of visual sense deprivation produced in a monochromatic environment devoid of a horizon—the so-called Ganzfeld Effect. Yeah, tell that to the folks at psychomanteum .org, where a guest mirror-gazer wrote:

> I prayed that God would let Blu [my cat] manifest
> if he wanted, and then I saw white swirling en-
> ergy. I felt like this may be Blu trying to show

himself. I watched this and then drifted into sleep
where I dreamed I was Blu chasing a rabbit.

Ganzfeld, my foot!

---

*So, Daryl, you may want to share some of this information
with Gladys.*

*As if! Ever since I've been hanging out with you guys, she'd
rather talk with Aunt Edna than with me.*

· V ·

Death as a Lifestyle Choice

✦

Did you ever get the feeling that you wanted to go,
But you wanted to stay,
But you wanted to go?

—Jimmy Durante as Banjo singing
in *The Man Who Came to Dinner*

"*Well,* finally—*a man who gets it!*"

11

Beating Death to the Punch Line

Jeez, Daryl, what's going on here? We admit we hardly know you, but you struck us as kind of an upbeat guy. So what's the deal with the gun barrel in your mouth?

Aargh . . . wigos . . . phip . . .

What's that you're saying, Daryl? We must say, it's hard to understand you with that thing in your mouth. Would you mind taking it out so we can talk this thing through?

Snrgg . . . filtm . . . snork . . .

Just hold on there, Daryl. Before you pull that trigger, would you mind answering a couple of questions of, well, a philosophical nature? We promise not to take up too much of your time—although from one perspective, you do have time to spare as compared to an eternity of nothingness. And, no, we're not going to try to talk you out of anything. No way— it's 100 percent your decision. We're just gathering data— you know, on the existential meaning of life, the morality of self-annihilation, exception clauses in your life insurance policy . . . that sort of thing.

First, we'd like to congratulate you on confronting what the twentieth-century French existentialist Albert Camus called the ultimate metaphysical question. As Al put it in the first lines of his essay *The Myth of Sisyphus,* **"There is but one truly serious philosophical problem, and that is suicide. Judging whether life is or is not worth living amounts to answering the fundamental question of philosophy."**[1]

What Al is saying is that once a person is conscious of suicide as an alternative to hanging in there, and that person chooses *not* to commit suicide—unlike, say, you, Daryl—he has consciously opted for life. His or her life, that is. He has taken the first step in accepting full responsibility for his existence. He *is* because he has chosen to be. In a sense, he has begun the lifelong task of creating himself.

Why, you may ask, would he want to do that? Actually, you, Daryl, flexing your trigger finger as you are, may already have answered that question to your own satisfaction: to wit, there is no good reason to want to continue creating your life. But on the off chance that you haven't given this question its full due, we suggest that now might be a good time to give it one more go-around.

Camus doesn't exactly offer an upbeat reason for choosing not to off yourself. He thought life was totally without meaning in any ordinary sense. In fact, the title character in *The Myth of Sisyphus* spends his days pushing a huge, heavy stone up the hill all day, only to have it roll back down. Not a real fulfilling life, eh? So you would think that Camus would agree with the graffito on the bathroom wall of our favorite existential coffee shop: **"Life's the joke; suicide's just the punch line."** But no, old Al comes out *against* suicide.

In the concluding sentence of the essay, Camus writes, "We must imagine Sisyphus happy." Why happy? Perhaps, like the antihero of Camus's *The Stranger* just before his execution, it is because he "opens his heart to the benign indifference of the universe." Like, life's absurd, so death's absurd—pretty funny, huh? It's all a cosmic joke, so what the hell, party on!

PEGGY LEE NAILS THE COSMIC JOKE

In her 1969 hit "Is That All There Is?" Ms. Lee spoke for an entire generation of absurdists who like to party.

When I was 12 years old, my father took me to a circus,
    the greatest show on earth.
There were clowns and elephants and dancing bears.
And a beautiful lady in pink tights flew high above our
    heads.
And so I sat there watching the marvelous spectacle.
I had the feeling that something was missing.
I don't know what, but when it was over,
I said to myself, "Is that all there is to a circus?"
Is that all there is, is that all there is?
If that's all there is, my friends, then let's keep dancing.

Let's break out the booze and have a ball,
If that's all there is.
I know what you must be saying to yourselves,
If that's the way she feels about it, why doesn't she just
    end it all?
Oh, no, not me. I'm in no hurry for that final
    disappointment,
For I know just as well as I'm standing here talking to
    you,
When that final moment comes and I'm breathing my
    last breath, I'll be saying to myself,
Is that all there is, is that all there is?
If that's all there is, my friends, then let's keep dancing.
Let's break out the booze and have a ball,
If that's all there is.

This existentialist anthem was written by none other than Jerry Leiber and Mike Stoller of "Hound Dog" fame. More surprisingly, Stoller says the song was inspired by the story "Disillusionment," by Thomas Mann.

If the party-on argument doesn't do it for you, Daryl, consider Camus's more serious take on suicide: to kill oneself is a failure of moral courage, an abdication of our responsibility to embrace the absurdity of life.

Does this resonate for you, Daryl?

Aargh . . . wigos . . . phip . . .

Are you back beating that dead horse again, Daryl? Or are you saying that you've been reading Goethe and you think suicide has an artistic, tortured-soul kind of panache *to it? God knows, the publication of Goethe's* The Sorrows of Young Werther *sparked a conflagration of romantic suicides all over Europe. That's late-eighteenth-century romanticism for you.*

Niggum . . . flirp . . .

Still with us, Daryl? We do wish you'd speak up. You're harder to understand than Demosthenes.

Oh, we guess you're saying that we don't comprehend your own individual plight, the particular set of circumstances that has led you to this pistol-in-mouth existential position. Ex-cuse us!

Seriously, Daryl, is it that you have a terminal illness that is causing you both physical pain and mental anguish? Is that why you want to end it all?

If so, it may be comforting to know that you are in good philosophical company. The ancient Stoics taught that the goal of life is "flourishing" or "living in agreement with nature." So if you're no longer flourishing, it's okay to take your own life. As Cicero put it, "When a man's circumstances contain a preponderance of things in accordance with nature, it is appropriate for him to remain alive; when he possesses or sees in prospect a majority of the contrary things, it is appropriate for him to depart from life."[2]

Who knew Dr. Kevorkian was a Stoic? Dr. K. (or, as some would have it, Dr. D.) also raises a more complex question of whether it's okay to help someone *else* commit suicide. Forget about the legal issue; morally, is assisted suicide a supreme act of love or is it perilously close to murder? Or, as situation ethicists would ask, "Doesn't it all depend on the situation?"

The Stoic Seneca even uses the words that the modern right-to-die folks have appropriated: "quality of life." Seneca wrote, "The wise man will live as long as he ought, not as long as he can. . . . [He] always reflects concerning the quality, not the quantity, of his life. As soon as there are many events in his life that give him trouble and disturb his peace of mind, he sets himself free."[3]

The contemporary philosopher Bill Maher put it more succinctly, if a bit more theologically: **"I believe Dr. Kevorkian is on to something. I think he's great. Because suicide is our way of saying to God, 'You can't fire me. I quit.' "**

A Special Case of Suicide: What Would You Die For?

I only regret that I have but one life to give for my country.   Nathan Hale

This Joan Rivers Diamond Dust Nail Collection is to die for.   The Shopping Channel

What would you die for?
Yes, we're talking to you, Daryl. We are appealing to

*"Before we try assisted suicide, Mrs. Rose,
let's give the aspirin a chance."*

your transcendental values. And to help you put the question in perspective, we offer you the following peer pressure:

According to one survey,[4] 68 percent of respondents in a multiple-choice poll answered that they would sacrifice their life for "My children," followed by a second-place tie at 48 percent between "My wife/husband" and "To save the world." Other responses were "Freedom of knowledge and learning for all people on earth" (40 percent), "Freedom and democracy" (36 percent), and "Freedom from censorship of news" (32 percent).

What's that, Daryl? You can't quite picture a situation where the choice would be between freedom of knowledge and learning for all people on earth, and your life?

Well, uh, let's say there was this cargo plane carrying fifty thousand complete sets of the Harvard Classics that was headed for the Congo and you are riding in the back with the books when you see the pilot drop dead at the controls . . . and . . . and . . . Uh, can we get back to you on this, Daryl?

Because there were only twenty-five respondents in this survey and each respondent chose an average of 2.7 things they would die for, we may want to label this particular group "High Die-ers." Yet great men and women throughout history have chosen death rather than abandon their cause.

It could be argued that most soldiers—suicide bombers and kamikaze pilots excepted—don't actually choose to die for their country so much as choose to *risk* death for their country, a very admirable but somewhat lower level of commitment. But Socrates, according to Plato's *Apology,* was offered acquittal if he would stop corrupting the youth of Athens with philosophy and refused, knowing that the alternative was death. How about Joan of Arc? Arguably, Joan's death was voluntary, in the sense that she must have known it was inevitable when she launched her career as a cross-dressing warrior in the fifteenth century.

Some philosophers have weighed in on the subject of giving one's life for a cause or an ideal or another person, but on the whole they've been a pretty uninspiring lot. Bertrand Russell, for instance, said, "I would never die for my beliefs because I might be wrong." French philosopher and leather queen Michel Foucault said, "To die for the love of boys: what could be more beautiful?" But Epicurus (the ancient Greek philosopher, not the recipe website) had a somewhat more profound take: he said a wise man is sometimes willing to die for his friend. That's a rather surprising sentiment from someone who argued that all our actions spring from the desire to maximize our own pleasure. That's partly because Eppy didn't really think death was a big whoop. "Death is nothing to us," he wrote, "since when we are, death has not come, and when death has come, we are not." Don't worry, be happy.

Today's assignment: in one hundred words or less, what would you die for? (N.B.: Because of limited stock, the Joan Rivers Diamond Dust Nail Collection is off the table.)

Nungy . . . snick . . . frup . . .

How's that, Daryl? Are you saying that's not it—you're in perfect health?

Okay, now we get it: You're depressed. You've had a bad run of it. Your stocks are tanking; your son, Daryl, Jr., is dating your sister; your wife has joined a free-love cult. You just want to say a final goodbye to the mess your life has turned into. We feel your pain.

But before we get into some moral issues about suicide that you may not have considered, here's a fable that addresses some practical issues you may have overlooked:

A schlemiel suspects his wife is cheating on him. One day he calls her at home and she answers out of breath. He plays it cool and drives home from work without her knowing. When he gets home, he sneaks up the stairs to the bedroom and busts open the door to find his wife having sex with the neighbor.

The schlemiel goes on a tirade, screaming, yelling, crying. Finally, he pulls out a gun and puts it to his own head and says, "I can't take this, I'm going to kill myself."

His wife and the neighbor just laugh.

And the schlemiel says, "Don't laugh, you're next!"

Where were we? Oh, yes, like we say, the choice is yours—that is, if you don't mind the fact that your final act is considered to be seriously immoral by some of the greatest thinkers who have ever lived. So take a moment and listen up.

Saint Augustine argued that suicide violates the commandment "Thou shalt not kill." He says that self-love is the gold standard of love in scripture: you shall love your neighbor as yourself. So the commandment not to kill clearly includes not killing yourself. Augustine says the Stoics' concept of flourishing is way too narrow. We should listen, he says, to the words of the apostle Paul and wait with patience and hope for the inexpressible happiness of the hereafter.

Saint Thomas Aquinas argues that suicide is contrary to natural law, the law of self-love, and he adds two other considerations that still resonate today in our arguments about suicide: first, suicide harms the community—we're guessing burial costs for starters; second, "it belongs to God alone to pronounce the sentence of death and life." The latter, or some natural-law variation of it, is reflected in our various state laws prohibiting suicide.

On the other hand, the British Enlightenment philosopher David Hume looked at the "community harm" argument from a secular point of view and found it unconvincing. He argued that there comes a time for many of us when our value to the community has become severely limited or when we have even become a liability to the community. "Suppose that it is no longer in my power to promote the interest of society, suppose that I am a burden to it, suppose my life hinders some person from being much more useful to society. In such cases, my resignation of life must not only be innocent, but laudable."[5] It is arguments like this that make Hume singularly unpopular with the seniors in Sun City.

Hume's German contemporary Immanuel Kant, however, saw suicide—and almost everything else—as a question of duty. Our rational will is the very source of our moral duty, he argued, so how can it ever be morally acceptable to destroy our rational will by suicide? That's the kind of question we'd expect in a book with a title like *Fundamental Principles of the Metaphysic of Morals*.

Perhaps we can shed a little light on the concept of duty with the following story:

A woman comes home early and finds her husband in bed with her best friend, Lucy. She stares incredulously at Lucy and shouts, "Me, I *have* to! But you??"

Daryl? Daryl?

Worggle . . . flurp . . . WHEW! I finally got that chunk of Milky Way out of my molar!

You were using a gun to pick your teeth?

I came out to walk the dog. Why would I carry a toothpick?

"We have no mandatory retirement age, Dave,
but under certain conditions we tend to encourage people to die."

· VI ·

Biotechnology:
Stop the Presses!

✦

Is death passé in the new millennium?
Is this book even necessary?
And more importantly,
if not, can I get my money back?

12

Immortality Through Not Dying

We don't know about you, Daryl, but we hope against hope that this whole death business is about to become a thing of the past. On this issue, we are of the same mind as Woody Allen, who famously said, **"I don't want to achieve immortality through my work. I want to achieve immortality through not dying."**

Imagine a world in which there would be no need for reincarnation or flitting about heaven with gauzy wings. You could toss out the whole catalogue of otherworldly, post-life-on-earth destination spots. Instead, you would just continue being a human being for eternity right here in Bayonne, New Jersey.

Among its many appeals, an infinite life span on earth offers familiarity; it's what you know, in fact, it's *all* you know, Daryl. You can hang on to all the stuff that has made you who you are, like your passion for the Mets and your knowledge that Guido's is the best pizza parlor in the neighborhood. All those otherworldly options for immortality require a leap of faith and some radical transformation, not to mention a drastic change of address and wardrobe.

You're just playing make-believe, right?

Not really, Daryl.

Until recently, biological immortality only existed in childhood fantasies and science-fiction novels. But recent discoveries in cell biology and artificial intelligence have given rise to serious scientists with advanced degrees who call themselves Biological Immortalists, researchers who foresee the possibility of genetic breakthroughs like cloning and stem cell therapy that will eliminate all the non-accidental causes of death. And there are also Cryobiological Preservation Immortalists, who are putting their money on freezing us while we wait for the breakthroughs. And then there are Cyber Immortalists, who see digitization of the human nervous system as the key to immortality. These people conceive of the possibility—nay, the *likelihood*—of a day in the not too distant future when they and their ilk can provide you with the means for eternal life more or less as you exist right now. The mind boggles, especially if it resides in a philosopher.

For one thing, it boggles with a whole new set of ethical problems like, Is there room for all these immortals on this planet, let alone in New Jersey? Is an infinite life span natural? Holy? Desirable? Affordable? Tedious? What are its implications for long-term bonds? For long-term relationships? Since we will have all the time in the universe, should we wait a few millennia before we get married?

This last question raises another problem.

Sean and Bridget had been seeing each other steadily for forty years. Then one day after a leisurely walk in the green hills of Kerry, Sean turned to Bridget and said, "You know, maybe we should get married."
Replied Bridget: "At our age, who'd have us?"

As we delve into the research that scientists are doing today at major universities on clone-immortality, cryo-immortality, and cyber-immortality, some metaphysical and epistemological questions also arise. Questions like, Am I still *me* if I'm only a defrosted brain? If I'm made entirely out of regenerated stem cells? If I only exist on a microchip? Who's the real me if there are four of me? Do I still need a condom for virtual sex?

But before we inquire further into a life without ever dying, let us take a moment to ponder just how long eternity is. Again we turn to Professor Allen for some insight: **"Eternity is very long, especially near the end."** Woody's point here is that just when you think you're nearing the end of eternity, they move the goalposts.

Sy comes home after his mother's funeral to try to put the place in order, and in the attic he finds an old trunk. Inside it, he discovers his father's World War II uniform. Sy tries it on and it's a little tight, but before taking it off, he puts his hand in the pocket and comes up with a piece of paper. It's a shoe repair ticket for Herman's on West Fifty-third, dated January 14, 1942. He can scarcely believe it. An unclaimed ticket almost seventy years old!

Weeks later, Sy happens to be in the area of West Fifty-third and wanders over to see where the shoe repair was. He can't believe his eyes; a shoe repair store is still there. He wanders in and tells the story of finding the ticket to the old man at the counter. The man says his name is Herman and he has owned the shop for seventy years. "Gimme the ticket!" barks Herman and wanders to the back of the shop.

Sy is amazed.

A moment later Herman shuffles back and says gruffly, "Okay, I've got your shoes. They'll be ready next Tuesday."

HIPPOCRATISY

From the point of view of medicine, the idea of preventing death is basically what doctors already aim for, so preventing death *forever* is just an extension of their Hippocratic protocol. Rare is the doc who sits you down and says, "We've knocked out your arteriosclerosis, so I'm happy to say you'll die of something else." On the contrary, we are always reading about medicine's glorious goal of wiping out the major causes of death—heart disease, stroke, and cancer—with no mention of the diseases waiting in line for the top spots on the mortality hit list. Thus do doctors *behave* as if they are immortalists, as if they can cure every ailment you will ever get.

HE WHO DIES WITH THE MOST BIRTHDAYS WINS

Living a long time always seems like more fun than living a short time, primarily because it's, well, *more*—more *life*, one of our favorite pastimes.

But as yuppies start to hit the three-score mark, living a long time has acquired an added value: it's an achievement, like getting a big job or selling the movie rights of your novel or seducing Angelina Jolie. As Michael Kinsley observes in his *New Yorker* essay about insights he has gained since being diagnosed with Parkinson's disease, "Mine Is Longer than Yours," competitive longevity is the aging Baby Boomers' final big contest. Writes Kinsley:

> **Of all the gifts that life and luck can bestow— money, good looks, love, power—longevity is the one that people seem least reluctant to brag about. In fact, they routinely claim it as some sort of virtue—as if living to ninety were primarily the result of hard work or prayer, rather than good genes and never getting run over by a truck."[1]**

Of course, there is a built-in paradox to this competition: The last man or woman to approach the Big Finish Line has no one left in his age group to one-up.

The comedian Steven Wright nailed the oat-bran

"Good news, Mrs. Bryant—I think we got it all."

munching Boomer set with his observation, "I feel sorry for people who don't drink or do drugs. Because some day they're going to be in a hospital bed, dying, and they won't know why."

THE PRIMORDIAL OOZE OOZES ON

From the point of view of evolutionary microbiology, an infinite life span is as familiar as a walk in the primordial ooze. Our germ line, the cells that produce our eggs and sperm, originated in this ooze, and we still carry this same prime cellular material around inside us. So, at the very least, microbiologists can say there are *parts* of us that are immortal. What this comes down to is that we have the capacity to reproduce our germ line indefinitely, which clearly is not the same as being a single complex organism that lives eternally, but hey, it's a step in the right direction.

Evolutionarily speaking, apparently where we humans went wrong is in the *way* we reproduce, the whole male/female, sperm/egg thing. Single-celled organisms reproduce by splitting their bodies into two biologically identical parts. After this reproductive split, two baby single cells are created. The original cell is no longer around to undergo aging, so it's reasonable to say that these species possess biological immortality. Not a bad trade-off for an unsexy sex life, but then again, single-celled organisms also miss out on tango lessons and Scrabble tournaments. Nonetheless, the bottom line remains that once we evolved our two-gender system for reproduction, this primordial form of immortality was lost to us. *Women—you can't live eternally with them, you can't live eternally without them.*

THE IMMORTALITY DOCTOR IS IN

There is a variety of immortality therapies currently out there, many with reasonably sound theoretical models, and some with promising ongoing research.

Take *stem cell replacement therapy*, a form of regenerative medicine that substitutes body components generated from undifferentiated cells (stem cells) for broken or dead components in a body. Most cells have a specific function—say, skin cells or brain cells—so once they've taken on their particular function (differentiation), they can't be tailored for any other function; but since stem cells are undifferentiated, they can develop into any kind of cell in the human body once they are "programmed" with the right instructions.

Stem cell therapy has already claimed success in inserting blood-producing cells into blood-damaged patients, and there is a host of other stem cell substitution therapies in the works, like spinal cord and partial brain replacements. On the drawing boards is a "totipotent" cell, a cell that could be inserted into a body and would then reconstruct any damaged or dead body component as needed, in the nick of time.

To get an idea of how this could result in immortality, picture a 1956 Chevy Bel Air that over time has had all of its parts replaced so that now it is exactly the same as when new except that it is not composed of any of its original material. Now imagine that you *are* that Bel Air.

Feelin' good, Daryl? Feeling like yourself? Do you even care?

Of course, the body regenerates cells on a regular basis, but only up to a point—death. Not so for the totipotent insert—it's on the job for eternity.

Which brings us to *telomerase therapy*, an immortality strategy that corrects the built-in death wish of our DNA. Scientists compare telomeres to the plastic tips on shoelaces in that they prevent chromosome ends from unraveling and sticking to one another, a scenario that could mess up an organism's genetic information and cause cancer and/or death. But there's a major downside to this function: each time a cell divides, the telomeres get shorter, and when they get too short, the cell is kaput. It's the ticking time-bomb inside all our chromosomes. This prompted the brainy folks at the genetic engineering company Geron to try to figure out how to put more *telos* in our telomeres.

In 1997, the Geron people discovered a gene that encodes a protein called telomerase that rewinds the "aging clock" at the ends of the chromosome. To date, they have had success only in petri dishes, where the opportunity for a rich and varied life is severely constricted. The Geron folks' guess is that in the future, telomerase therapy will stop aging indefinitely, but most scientists do not think it can *reverse* aging. Keep this in mind if you are seventy-five years old, like Malcolm:

Malcolm was taking a walk when he saw a frog in the gutter. He was startled to hear the frog suddenly say to him, "Old man, if you kiss me, I'll turn into a beautiful princess. I'll be yours forever, and we can make mad passionate love every night."

Malcolm bent down and put the frog in his pocket and continued walking.

The frog said, "Hey, I don't think you heard me. I said if you kiss me, I'll turn into a beautiful princess and we can make passionate love every night."

Malcolm said, "I heard you all right, but at my age I'd rather have a talking frog."

Another biotechnological strategy for prolonging life indefinitely goes by the space-age moniker *nanorobotics*. These are devices that range in size from 0.1 to 10 micrometers, the same scale as the body's molecular components. Working in a way similar to stem cell replacement, nanorobots could be inserted into the body for perpetual search-and-repair missions at the molecular level. Not only is the immortality doctor in, he's *inside* you. Nanorobotic scientists believe they will have workable models in the next twenty to thirty years. If you don't expect to live until then, not to worry—cryonic therapy is right around the corner.

Cryogenics is as old as Clarence Birdseye, the Father of Frozen Foods, who hatched his multimillion-dollar idea when, as a fur trader in Labrador, he discovered that the Eskimos routinely froze fish and caribou for later consumption. *Yum*, said Clarence, after downing a defrosted dolphin.

"You're not fired, Harris.
I'm just having you frozen till things pick up again."

Okay, so Birdseye didn't invent cryonics, but the principle he discovered lives on in laboratory freezers around the world. Cryonic preservation is the process of preserving cells or whole tissues by cooling them to sub-zero temperatures, temperatures at which all biological activity, including any reaction that could lead to cell death, is arrested.

These days it is routine to freeze sperm, human eggs, and embryos for later defrosting and use. So why not freeze entire human beings for later use, say for a future time when the diseases that once threatened a body now have a cure?

Well, for one thing, some sticky practical problems arise from the fact that the best way to freeze a body for future re-animation is when that body is still alive. This can be a major dilemma if you are in the middle of a major financial transaction or a wild love affair at the time of your optimum freezing point. So far, the folks who have opted for full or partial (i.e., brain) freezing have chosen the chancier route of being frozen as soon *after* the instant of death as possible. We consider that a choice based on lack of faith.

Another problem with the cryogenic route is also related to faith, the faith that some person in the future—possibly somebody who never knew you—will decide it's worth her time and expense to thaw you out and fix whatever ailed you. Exactly what is going to motivate her? Perhaps lawyers could work out a contract that would impel this future thawer to open your freezer door, but somehow it doesn't feel like a sure thing. Unfrozen people change, you know.

A guy buys an expensive talking parrot that has a large vocabulary. This bird is quoting Shakespeare and Dylan Thomas all the way home to the guy's house, but once inside the bird lets loose with a tirade of foul language. "You #@&*! You call this @%# a house?" On and on he goes, swearing like a sailor, and whenever the guy tells him to stop, he just gets more foulmouthed. Finally, the guy says, "Okay, into the cooler for you until you can talk decent," and he grabs the bird and stuffs him in the freezer. After several minutes of ranting, the bird suddenly falls silent, and the guy opens the freezer door.

The parrot hops out onto the man's shoulder. "I am so sorry, Master, please forgive me," he coos. "By the way, what did the chicken do?"

The Grim Reaper's Unemployment Problem and Other Considerations

Among the more down-to-earth questions raised by the possibility of down-on-earth immortality are the moral considerations of Environmental Ethics, a recent subdivision of Applied Ethics—most pressingly, *Where the hell are we going to keep all these immortals?* In a world already stressed by scarce resources for a burgeoning population, what are we going to do when our basic population stabilizer—the Grim Reaper—hangs up his scythe?

The obvious solution is to cut down at the other end—reduce or even terminate the production of new bodies to make room for very old bodies.

Arguably the greatest political satirist in the English language, Jonathan Swift, submitted his own version of this particular solution to overpopulation in his famous 1729 essay, *A Modest Proposal: For Preventing the Children of Poor People in Ireland from Being a Burden to Their Parents or Country, and for Making Them Beneficial to the Publick*. In, well, Swiftian prose, Swift proposed that the Irish reverse their economic misfortunes by selling the children of the poor as food for the rich. Well, that *is* one way to do it.

Reform Judaism attacks the immortality-sans-reproduction solution in a more earnest manner in a poignant meditation for the Yom Kippur (Day of Atonement) memorial service:

> If some messenger were to come to us with the offer that death should be overturned, but with the one inseparable condition, that birth should also cease; if the existing generation were given the chance to live forever, but on the clear understanding that never again would there be a child, or a youth, or first love, never again new persons with new hopes, new ideas, new achievements; ourselves for always and never any others—could the answer be in doubt?

Of course, even if the prospect of biological immortality were entirely realistic, the prospect that it would be available to one and all is totally improbable. Most of the world's popu-

lation cannot afford or obtain basic medical care, so the possibility of search-and-heal nanorobots being available to anyone who asks for them strains credulity. The far greater
likelihood is that nanorobots or telomerase therapy would be
reserved for the likes of Warren Buffett, Bill Gates, and Tiger
Woods, folks who can afford an expensive hobby like Eternal
Existence.

If this sounds patently unfair, that's because it patently is.
It gives the concept "survival of the fittest" an entirely new
meaning—*eternal* survival of the fittest.

STILL CRAZY AFTER ALL THESE EONS

On the fuzzy border between phenomenology and psychology lie questions about how biological immortality would
change our experience of being human. Are these changes
that we really bargained for?

Say you've got nanorobots busily repairing all the decay-
ing parts of your mortal coil so that disease and normal wear
and tear no longer lead to the Big Sleep. Still, those busy little
robots have their limits; they're no help if you are obliterated
by a grand piano falling out of a building or if you happen to
hitch a ride with Thelma and Louise on their trip to the Grand
Canyon. Now the *only* way you can die is by such a catastro-
phe. What's this going to do to your mind-set? Your situation
is no longer whether you are going to die now or later; *it's
whether you're going to die at all*. You might say the stakes have

"Better safe than sorry, son."

just gotten bigger—*way* bigger. Under the new setup, won't we be prone to live lives that are totally devoid of risk—say, sequestered in a bomb-proof box buried under the ground?

ENOUGH ALREADY

The problem of *ennui*—that's Existentialist French for extreme boredom with life accompanied by lots of weary shrugs and sighs—reaches a new dimension with the prospect of eternal life in, say, the same old café in Saint-Germain-des-Prés. In his essay "The Makropulos Case: Reflections on the Tedium of Immortality," the twentieth-century Cambridge moral philosopher Sir Bernard Williams argues that death is necessary if life is to remain interesting. Williams's reference point is the play *The Makropulos Affair* by the Czech writer Karel Čapek (and the subsequent opera by Czech composer Leos Janáček), in which the heroine is granted an extraordinarily long life (342 years and counting) by way of an alchemic elixir. But by the play's end she decides against re-upping for yet more centuries because she has realized that perpetual life only offers endless apathy. Writes Williams, "Her unending life has come to a state of boredom, indifference and coldness. Everything is joyless."

How so? Williams believes that after a person has lived a certain number of years (this number apparently varies from one individual to another) she is incapable of having new experiences—it's the old been-there-done-that problem. *Ipso facto*, she becomes bored out of her gourd. The good life, says

Williams, is one that ends before repetition and boredom inevitably set in.

Of course, there are some, like the comedian Emo Phillips, who argue that appreciating endless repetition is an acquired taste:

> "A friend of mine gave me a Philip Glass record. I listened to it for five hours before I realized it had a scratch on it."

The nineteenth-century German philosopher Friedrich Nietzsche raised the boredom question to a new level with his notion of Eternal Recurrence. According to Freddy N., the best symbol of the futility of an eternal destiny is history repeating itself over and over, *ad infinitum*. To some, like Woody Allen, this prospect seems worthy of an eternal *Oy!* Says Professor Allen, "[Nietzsche] said that the life we lived we're going to live over again the exact same way for eternity. Great. That means I'll have to sit through the Ice Capades again."

Think again, says the Fredster. Don't let eternal recurrence get you down—rise above it! The heroism of the Nietzschean Superman is shown by his ability to assert his will to power *in spite of* that futility. Well, fine for the Superman! But what about ordinary folks, like Lois Lane and Jimmy Olsen, not to mention you, Daryl, and us? For us, eternal recurrence sounds more like *Groundhog Day,* and that profound exchange of dialogue that has sent shivers down many a moviegoer's spine:

Bill Murray character: "What would you do if every day was the same, and nothing you did ever mattered?"

New friend in a bar: "That about sums it up for me."

TRY TO REMEMBER THAT DAY IN SEPTEMBER

The 1998 Japanese film *After Life* gives Nietzsche's idea of Eternal Recurrence a novel and surprisingly thought-provoking interpretation: Newly dead clients shamble into a drab office building where social workers inform them they have three days to select their most cherished memory. Once this memory is chosen, it will become the *only* experience each new arrival has for all of eternity. *Talk about decisions that have big-time implications for the future!*

The setup seems Hollywood "high-concept," but in the hands of director Hirokazu Koreeda it is a profound exploration of—not to put too fine a point on it—*the meaning of life.*

Should I choose the experience that is most emblematic of my entire life? The most dramatic one? The most intense one? (Many of the old men start off by choosing their most fiery sexual experience, but upon reflection decide that an eternal orgasm lacks a certain nuance.)

Along the way, one young girl wants to relive a day at Disneyland, only to reconsider after a social worker gently informs her that thirty others had made the same choice that year; a tortured middle-aged man chooses the breeze felt on a tram ride the day before a school summer vacation; an old woman opts for her memory of dancing for her older brother's friends in a red dress. Banal as their final decisions may sound, the deliberations that precede them are deeply moving.

TIME FOR SOMETHING COMPLETELY DIFFERENT

Tedious as *ennui* may be, we're not ready to throw out the prospect of an infinite number of experiences, no matter how repetitious they are. It still sounds a lot better than the eternal cessation of *all* experiences.

For a radical solution to this eternal desire for more experience we turn to the contemporary Viennese-Australian polymath Manfred Clynes, who is known for personally packing several lifetimes into one: he has made his mark as a neurophysiologist, inventor, and concert pianist. So leave it to Manfred to come up with a strategy for extending life indefinitely without actually adding any "clock time" to our life span.

Clynes proposes that we expand life, not by adding seconds onto the end, but by speeding up our *time-consciousness* so that each second has way more "moments" in it. He informs us that computers have a certain "tick rate," the speed at which they process information, and that rate, in theory, can be speeded up indefinitely, so that one day we, too, may be able to use

> an expanding time consciousness, a speeding-up adjustment using nanotechnology, or picotechnology; thinking could be say 10,000 times faster than we are used to. What would happen then? A year would last 10,000 years. The seasons would not change for 2,500 years. Aging will be eliminated as we know it.[2]

It makes us wonder what the *experience* of living in this super-fast lane would be like. Would it merely be like the guy who took a speed-reading course and reported: **"I read *Moby Dick* in its entirety in twenty-five minutes! It's about a whale."**

Or would our enjoyment of the book simply speed up too, Dr. C.? And what exactly would that mean?

Oh, Daryl, is this your wife? Yes, Mrs. Frumkin, you have a question?

What does speeded-up time consciousness do to foreplay?

Uh, maybe that's a discussion you and Daryl would like to have in private.

Meantime, let's get back to Manfred's jam-packed life. Where does *meaning* fit into his picture?

In David Ives's ten-minute play *Time Flies*, Horace and

May, two mayflies, fall madly in love at first sight. *("I was born just this morning." "So was I.")* They watch a nature show on their first date and discover they have a life span of only one day: their lives are already half over! After some moments of confusion and panic, they decide to make the most of what they have and fly to Paris, where they anticipate a dandy time, a happy ending, as it were.

Horace and May have managed to find meaning in their very short lives, despite—or maybe because of—their awareness of the end. Would their lives have been richer with the aid of speed-living? What if they could have crammed London *and* Paris into the same time? How about London, Paris, and Rio? Okay, throw in Vegas, that's our last offer, and you get to assume that Céline Dion isn't sold out.

Or consider a Buddhist monk who spends 90 percent of his waking hours sitting in the lotus position emptying his mind of all thoughts except for one: communing with the Oneness of the Cosmos. Not a whole lot of variety of experiences for this chap. Does this mean he's having a blah life?

Clynes is raising none other than the perennial phenomenological question of the relativity of lived time. One man's (or turtle's) minute of living is another man's (or turtle's) month of living, so just who or which is having the richer life?

Some turtles went on a picnic. It took them ten days to get there, and when they arrived, they realized they'd forgotten the bottle opener, so they told the littlest one to go back for it. He said, "No, as soon as I go, you'll eat the sandwiches." They promised him they wouldn't, so he left. Ten days passed, twenty days, thirty days. Finally, they were so hungry, they decided to eat the sandwiches. As soon as they took a bite, the little turtle came out from behind a rock and said, "See? That's why I'm not going."

SEND IN THE CLONES

If speed-living sounds too labor-intensive, consider the sexiest—if totally asexual—biological technique for immortality through not dying: *Clone yourself.* In fact, not only clone yourself, but clone yourself as a very young person; then as you age, do it again . . . and again . . . and again, *ad infinitum.*

Of all the biotechnical schemes for creating human immortals, human cloning not only appears to be eminently possible in the near term, but may very well have happened already, although nobody's telling. (That's because it's against the law.) Certainly the technique, known as somatic cell nuclear transfer, has already produced Dolly the sheep. (Rumors that Dolly keeps muttering to herself "Every day feels like the same old shit" have been unsubstantiated.)

Here's how cloning works: the cytoplasm (the material between the nuclear and cell membranes) is removed from a donor's egg cell; then another cell with the genetic material that will be cloned is melded to the original egg cell. *Voila!*— an identical copy of the original is in the cooker.

One reason we're sure that human cloning is possible is that it already happens frequently in nature: it's called having identical twins. Identical twins are produced when a single

fertilized egg splits into two cell masses and becomes two people with identical DNA. They are only confused with frater-
nal twins (two different eggs that are fertilized separately but
come to full term from the same womb at the same time) by
people like Merle Haggard, who, when asked if his twin
nephews were identical, replied, **"One's identical, but the
other don't look like anybody."**

JOKES NOT WORTH CLONING

Human cloning has produced almost as many bad
jokes—mostly about cloning's parallels to redneck reproductive practices—as the subject of sex with aliens.
But one bit of wit stands out from the herd:

> The cloning of humans is on most of the lists of
> things to worry about from Science, along with
> behavior control, genetic engineering, trans-
> planted heads, computer poetry and the unre-
> strained growth of plastic flowers.[3]

But does cloning create a perfect replica of the original?
Ask a natural identical twin: she doesn't think she is the same
person as her exact DNA copy for the simple reason that she's
had different experiences from her copy. She's had different
influences on the development of her personality; she has different memories, different reference points; she's made differ-

Savings based on single copy price $5.00. Offer
valid in U.S. and Canada only. Canadian orders
add $30 per year in U.S. funds (GST included). THE
WEEK publishes three double issues, each counts
as two of 51 issues in an annual subscription. Offer
valid on new subscriptions only.

BUSINESS REPLY MAIL

FIRST-CLASS MAIL   **PERMIT NO 22**   **TAMPA FL**

POSTAGE WILL BE PAID BY ADDRESSEE

THE WEEK

PO BOX 62290
TAMPA FL 33663-2901

ent connections, found different meanings. In developmental psychology, this provides a fascinating experimental model for investigating the old nature vs. nurture conundrum, as in the pair of developmental psychologists who had twins: one they called John, and the other, Control.

So just how identical do identical twins turn out to be? Not so much. Certainly not so much that in critical situations an outside observer can't distinguish one from the other.

Reggie married one of a pair of identical twins. Less than a year later, he was in court filing for a divorce.

"Okay," the judge said, "tell the Court why you want a divorce."

"Well, Your Honor," Reggie began, "every once in a while my sister-in-law would come over for a visit, and because she and my wife are so identical-looking, every once in a while I'd end up making love to her by mistake."

"Surely there must be some difference between the two women," the judge said.

"You'd better believe there is a difference, Your Honor. That`s why I want the divorce," he replied.

More critical for our purposes are the *experiential* differences between identical twins.

Consider these two men sitting next to each other in a Boston pub. After a while, one looks at the other and says, "I can't help but think, from listening to you, that you're from Ireland." The other guy responds proudly, "Yes, that I am!" The first guy says, "So am I! And whereabouts from Ireland might you be?" The other guy answers, "I'm from Dublin, I am." The first guy responds, "Sure and begorra, and so am I! And what street did you live on in Dublin?" The other guy says, "A lovely little area it was, I lived on McCleary Street in the old central part of town." The first guy says, "Faith and it's a small world, so did I! And to what school would you have been going?" The second guy says, "St. Mary's." The first guy gets really excited, and says, "And so did I. Tell me, what year did you graduate?" The other guy answers, "Well, now, I graduated in 1964." The first guy exclaims, "The Good Lord must be smiling down upon us! I can hardly believe our good luck at winding up in the same bar tonight. Can you believe it, I graduated from St. Mary's in 1964 my own self." About this time, another guy walks into the bar, sits down, and orders a beer. The bartender walks over shaking his head and mutters, "It's going to be a long night, the Murphy twins are drunk again."

So if you clone yourself in an attempt to achieve biological immortality, how do you go about creating a copy that has an identical self? How do you make your clone "you" when he says "me"?

Easy, reply the Clone Immortalists, you simply download the entire contents of your nervous system—memories, sensitivities, voting pattern on *American Idol*, the whole "you" package—into your clone's neural equipment, onto its/his hard drive, as it were. In this way, it/he will answer to your name, laugh at your favorite jokes, vote for the skinny kid with the falsetto on *American Idol,* and enthusiastically make love to your wife, Gladys.

So there you are standing next to this perfect clone of you who has had your entire nervous system downloaded into his own nervous system. Ask him how he feels about having sex in a dogsled and he gives the exact, nuanced reply that you would. Tickle him in that special spot just behind his right earlobe and he chortles just the way you do when tickled there. Ask him if he believes in God, and again he responds with the identical equivocal response that you would. Even ask him who he is and he'll say, "*Du*-uh! I'm Daryl Frumkin. Who the hell are *you?*"

To say the least, your clone has an awful lot in common with you—same reflexes, opinions, knowledge, memories. In fact, it's hardly a stretch to say that he has the exact same mental software and remembered experiences that you have. So why this nagging doubt that Daryl Frumkin, the clone, is not the same as you, Daryl Frumkin, the original?

It has to do with something we call our "self"—a phenomenon we think of as distinct from our "mind" or even our "soul." And no matter which of the myriad forms of immortality we long for, it always comes down to this entity we call our "self" that we want to preserve for all time. Above all, that's the thing that we want to stick around for eternity.

But what is this thing called *self*?

Back in the seventeenth century, René Descartes opened the oven door to this question when he tried to doubt the reality of everything. In his *Meditations on First Philosophy,* he even went so far as to imagine an Evil Demon who is zapping an ersatz "reality" into our minds without our realizing it. Descartes was doing pretty well at his doubting experiment when he came up against the fact that he couldn't doubt his own doubting. He famously exclaimed, "I think, therefore I am," meaning, "I doubt, therefore I can't doubt my own existence (as a doubter)."

Flash forward to the late nineteenth and early twentieth centuries when the German philosopher Edmund Husserl saw that Descartes had revealed a whole new dimension to understanding human experience with his insight that there needs to be an experience of an "I-myself" for my other experiences to be experienced as "mine." So Ed began to examine this experience of self to see what else he could figure out about it.

One thing he saw was that I don't just experience this self as sitting there like a day-old pizza; I experience my self as connecting my experiences to each other and giving them coherence and meaning. My self is the "perspective point" that gives organization to my experiences. We experience time, for example, as the "living present." As an experience, time isn't just a straight line of discrete moments or a present-point racing along a track. Our present is always a knitting together of our memories of the past and our anticipation of the future. We always experience our self as continuous through time.

BEAM ME UP, DR. EINSTEIN

Teleportation, today's hottest new physics project, has already demonstrated that it is possible to instantaneously reposition objects or elementary particles from Point A to Point B without these items ever sailing through space. So far, "exact" teleportation has only been accomplished with atoms and photons. Exact teleportation seems to be a sort of "cut and paste" operation: you cut a photon on this end and paste it somewhere else.

What's that, Daryl? You say the text you cut on your computer isn't the same text, the same physical marks, that pop up when you click on "Paste"? They just look the same?

Well, you may have a point there. But consider this: neither of the "texts" on your computer is ultimately real. They're both just translations of zeros and ones (switches either off or on) in your computer circuitry. And what would it mean to say that the zeros and ones at the end point aren't the *same* as the zeros and ones on the near end? Zeros and ones don't exist in space at all!! If you've seen one zero or one one, you've seen them all. Pretty wiggy stuff, huh? In any case, you've zeroed in on the notion of "inexact" teleportation.

Inexact teleportation takes encoded information about an object and zaps it from one point to another; then, using the teleported information as a blueprint, the object is perfectly reconstructed at the end point. That's pretty much what you were implying happens with "cut and paste." Inexact teleportation apparently depends on a property of atomic particles called "entanglement" wherein particles that are far apart are sometimes naturally twinned, with the properties of one affecting the other. As one physicist put it, "You tickle one atomic particle and the other one laughs." Helpfully, Einstein described this property as "spooky action at a distance." Thanks for the heads-up, Al.

Needless to mention, there is already a lot of chatter in the physics community about teleporting a human being, most promisingly by inexact teleportation. In other words, *cloning at a distance.*

Oh, did we mention that the original object—say, you, Daryl Frumkin, of Bayonne, New Jersey—gets obliterated in the process? Not to worry, the teleported you, Daryl Frumkin of Gusev Crater, Mars, is doing just fine, thank you.

And that brings us back to Husserl's point. He and the other phenomenologists argued that I don't experience my environment as merely registering on my mind, as if it were a film (or, nowadays, a computer screen). The phenomenologists said that this leaves out a crucial step. An integral element in all my experiences is that I experience them as "belonging" to what they called a "phenomenological self" (or, as most of us call it, "me"). I continuously have the experience of this "I" who is the center-point of all of my other experiences, the point where all my perceptions, thoughts, meanings, and intentions intersect.

We think Husserl and his followers have nailed what it is that we all hope has a life beyond the grave. It's our self! Any immortality that falls short of preserving a continuity of "self" consciousness just isn't the kind of immortality we hanker for.

CLINGING TO OUR SELF

Interestingly, Husserl is echoing an idea that Gautama the Buddha put forth in the sixth century B.C. Gautama taught that we *construct* our experience of self by sort of picking and choosing from the "five heaps of clinging." Those heaps, or *skandhas*, are our sense of our physical form, our sensations, our thoughts, our habits, and our awareness. Out of these we weave a self, and with that self we interact with what's left over—a world. No wonder he thought they were both illusory.

Okay, back to Daryl Frumkin, the clone. Does this Daryl have a "phenomenological self"? Does he/it have continuity of consciousness? If we just dissolve into our experiences with no central organizing perspective, *who*, exactly, is at home? Who is it who has survived? Does having our personalities downloaded to a clone preserve the self-awareness we'll need in order to *experience* immortality? (And if we can't experience that we are "immortal," why'd we go to all this trouble?)

But, hey, maybe we can just download your phenomenological self too, Daryl. Would this self then be you? Would *you* think it was you? More importantly, would your clone think he was Daryl? And if so, who would he think *you* are?

As for us, we've asked our clones to communicate the answer to you after our download. But then again, can you trust a couple of clones who say they're us?

ME, MYSELF, AND iPOD

Taking the neural downloading game plan to its ultimate end point is cyber-immortality. Proponents of this plan are quick to point out that human bodies are made out of flimsy stuff that is always prone to wear and tear, not to mention falling pianos. So why not tuck our entire "self" onto computer chips where it can go on "living" and even engage in new (cyber) experiences forever? This approach gives new meaning to the expression "chip off the old block."

If living entirely as a "mind" has a familiar ring to philosophy types, it's probably because Bishop George Berkeley, the eminent eighteenth-century British empiricist, posited a similar idea in the pre-computer-chip era when he famously said, *"Esse est percipi"* ("To be is to be perceived"). Bishop B. was saying that there are no *substantial* "things" out there, only our perceptions, which we *call* "things." At first blush, it seems to be a solipsistic universe, because all we can be absolutely sure of is what's inside our minds. But of course this raised the question of where our sensory input comes from if not from "objects," and the churchman had a snappy reply: God sends us sensory data all the time from On High. It's kinda like cosmic spam. Substitute a phrase like "software engineer who programmed our chip-brains to receive and process ever-new and lively data" for "God" and Berkeley's theory lives on.

Cyber Immortalist Michael Treder suggests **"making a digital copy of our brain and downloading all the information into a robot. This method has the advantage of being able to preserve a backup copy of our personality, as insurance against the remote possibility that something catastrophic might destroy our robot body. This really would make us effectively immortal, as we could store copies of ourselves in places all over the solar system, the galaxy, or eventually even beyond."**[4]

Not to be party poopers, but we do have a philosophical question we'd like answered before downloading. The twentieth-century British philosopher C. D. Broad points out that our consciousness of a thing is different from the sum of our information about the physical properties of that thing. The added element is the "what-it's-like" aspect of experience. We could know everything there is to know about the physical properties of beer and its interactions with everything else, including our taste buds, and that still wouldn't tell us how beer tastes. We still wouldn't know what the experience of tasting beer is. Your local bartender probably could have told you the same thing, so C.D. needed an ersatz Latin name for these "what-it's-like" experiences to give his observation a little *panache,* so he called them *qualia.*

Suppose we program two robots, Dusty and Lily, to have sex. Let's listen in and hear what they have to say to each other:

DUSTY: Was it good for you too, Lily?

LILY: Omigod, yes, Dusty. It was wonderful. It's always wonderful, Dusty.

DUSTY: Uh . . . I know you must have had other relationships, Sweet Lips, and I'm a fool to bring this up, but I'm just hoping ours compares, you know, *favorably?*

LILY: Of course, darling. I've never known love like ours.

DUSTY: That's the way it computes for me too! But tell me what you're feeling, Angel Face.

LILY: Well, my numbers skyrocket when we're together.

DUSTY: Yeah, yeah, I know, mine too. But what does it *feel* like for you?

LILY: I behave atypically, Dusty. I block out my other software.

DUSTY: Yes, yes, I understand, my pet. But what is this crazy thing called love? Can you name it? Can you tell me what you're feeling right now?

LILY: Could you rephrase the question? I'm not computing it.

DUSTY: For godssake, Lily! I don't think you really love me.

LILY: Of course I love you, Dusty. All my bulbs light up when you waddle into view.

DUSTY: That's just a mechanical thing, Lily! I can get a mechanical reaction from a pinball machine! Don't you see? It's your *love* I want! Oh, hell, I'll catch you later. I'm going out to run some beer-drinking software with the boys.

LILY: *(sighs)* I'll be here, Dusty. I guess I'm just programmed that way.

What the hell is your point, guys?

Well, Daryl, you could obviously program Dusty and Lily to ask and answer Dusty's questions. You could even program Lily to read her own data, compute how the event had scored against certain criteria or as compared with sex with other robots, and answer accordingly. But if Dusty's asking Lily about her *qualia*, won't Lily's answer be purely mechanical?

What's that, Daryl? That's the sort of answer you often get from Gladys too?

Now if we're going to "extend our life" by "downloading our personality," we want to know: Are we going to be able to download our *qualia*? And how would that work exactly? We don't know about you, but we're not going anywhere without our *qualia*. It just wouldn't be the same.

We know not what course others may take, but as for us, give us our *qualia* or give us death.

Qualia, schmalia! I'll take living in Bayonne for all of eternity even if I'm made out of spare parts or I'm frozen or I'm no bigger than a computer chip. Whatever, it sure beats the alternative! So thanks for the heads-up, guys! Toodleoo!

Hold it right there, Daryl! You haven't been listening carefully. Maybe these biotechnological schemes are promising, but not yet! They're still on the drawing boards. Meantime—brace yourself for this one, friend—the very best possibility is that you are a member of the last generation to die!

Omigod! I think I'm having a heart attack!

· VII ·

The End

✦

It ain't over until the fat lady sings.
Oops, she's singing.

{ 13 }

The End

Daryl! It's been a long time! What are you doing here?

What am I doing here? I work here. This is my funeral parlor.

Geez, we didn't know you were in this business.

You never asked. Say, why are you guys here?

For our dear old pal, Freddy Moriarty.

Oh, yes, old Freddy. I was just getting my schtick ready for his service.

Schtick?

Yeah, it's my new thing. Hanging out with you guys got me thinking. Here I'd been dealing with dead people all my life and I'd never really thought about, you know, deathiness.

But schtick?

Grab a seat. I'm just going on stage. You can check me out.

Good afternoon, ladies and gentlemen. You may have noticed the other service going on down the hall. It's for the man who invented the Hokey-Pokey. Actually, he's been a bit of a challenge. When we laid him in his coffin, we put his left leg in. That's when the trouble started.

A lot of you have asked me about the furniture here in the room. It goes back to Louis the fourteenth. That is, unless I pay Louis by the thirteenth.

We buried a man last week who drowned in a boating accident. Yeah, he had rented a boat, and they kept yelling at him from the dock, "Boat number 99, your time is up. Boat number 99, your time is up. Please return to the dock." They called several times, but there was no answer. Then they remembered they only had 75 boats—there wasn't any boat number 99. That's when they realized boat 66 was in trouble.

My staff is out right now, picking up the body of a crossword puzzle master. The family wants him buried 6 down and 3 across.

But if I can get serious for just a minute, folks, I've been reading a lot of philosophers lately on the meaning of life and death and the hereafter. They have all these different theories about this stuff, and to tell the truth, they don't take much notice of the way ordinary people like you and me and old Freddy here think about these things.

But there's this one guy who stands out from the pack, an American philosopher from a hundred years ago named William James. He said a couple of things that hit the old coffin nail right on the head. Like he said philosophers aren't a whole lot different from you and me when it comes to how they arrive at their beliefs about the meaning of it all. He said all of us get our answers to the big questions sort of by intuition. He called it our "dumb sense of what life honestly and deeply means"—and he didn't mean "dumb" as a put-down, either. Whether we're professional philosophers or just ordinary *schlubs* like Freddy and me, we mostly rely on our gut for our sense of what it's all about. James said we all have our own way of "just sensing and feeling the total push and pressure of the cosmos."

Now some philosophers, and I'm not mentioning any names—mostly because I can't pronounce them—try to hide the fact that they *feel* their way to the Big Answers just like the rest of us do. They spin out all kinds of fancy, impersonal reasons for coming to their conclusions, but the way they *really* got there is they trusted their gut in the first place, just like the rest of us. But because they wanted an impressive philosophy that matched what they felt in their guts, they constructed it out of their heads. And here's where they got a little sneaky, for my money: they kinda cherry-picked the universe for evidence that backed up what their gut told them to start with, and they ignored anything that didn't jibe with it. Dirty pool, if you ask me.

Here's another thing this James guy said that rang a few bells in the tower for me. He said that when the facts out there aren't really clear—you know, front and center in flashing neon—we're free to choose the philosophy that seems best to us. He's talking about the Meaning of It All here—life, death, the whole enchilada. So, if a heaven in the clouds seems to you to be the way the universe is pushing you, then, hey, what's the problem? Who am I to say you're wrong? I honestly hope you get there, and in fact I hope I can drop by up there and see you sometime. Maybe we can kick back, have a beer, and talk. Like I sometimes do with my new friends back there in the last row. Yeah, those two old guys.

Oh, one last thing. There was this other American guy who lived a while back by the name of Thornton Wilder. He was a playwright, and in the third act of his play *Our Town*, the young heroine, Emily, has died in childbirth and she's given a chance to relive one day in her life. She chooses her twelfth birthday. At first she is overcome with joy reliving this day, but pretty quickly she realizes how fast life passes by and how much of life she took for granted. "We don't even have time to look at one another!" she cries. At the end of her visit, she turns to the Stage Manager and asks, "Doesn't anyone ever realize life while they live it? Every, every minute?" And the Stage Manager says, "No. Saints and poets, maybe; they do some."

Thanks for coming, everybody. I know you came to see Freddy and not me, but Freddy's indisposed. I appreciate your giving me a listen. Oh, one more story—last one, I promise.

So Heidegger and a hippo stroll up to the Pearly Gates and Saint Peter says, "Listen, we've only got room for one more to-day. So whoever of the two of you gives me the best answer to the question 'What is the meaning of life?' gets to come in."

And Heidegger says, "To think Being itself explicitly requires disregarding Being to the extent that it is only grounded and interpreted in terms of beings and for beings as their ground, as in all metaphysics."

But before the hippo can grunt one word, Saint Peter says to him, "Today's your lucky day, Hippy!"

Good night, everybody! Safe trip home! You too, Freddy.

ACKNOWLEDGMENTS

∽∞∾

There are a number of people on this side of the Great Divide we wish to thank for their help and support: our beloved agent, Julia Lord; our super-smart editor, Stephen Morrison; his ever-vigilant right-hand assistant, Becca Hunt; and our publicist at Penguin, Yen Cheong. As to those on the other side of the Great Divide, we'll get to you shortly.

Back in our student days, two teachers braved the scorn of their analytic colleagues and introduced us to the big, murky questions we really wanted to hear about. Those teachers were the late John Wild and the later Paul Tillich. It was a privilege to study with them.

Far and away our best source of jokes is Gil Eisner, a human repository of classic gags. Thanks, Gil. Also thanks to Joan Griswold and Paddy Spence for a couple of goodies.

We also tip our jester cap to some of the most inventive comedic writers we've ever read: Groucho Marx, Woody

Allen, Emo Phillips, Steven Wright, Merle Haggard, and Martin Heidegger. For pointing us to movies about Heaven we'd never heard of, thanks to Jack Nessel.

As to our wives, Eloise and Freke, and our daughters, Esther and Samara, what can we say? You are nice. *Way* nice.

Many years ago, when Freke's father, the late Reverend Jan Vuijst, was on his deathbed, he spent a private moment with me (Danny). Among his last words was a statement I will never forget: "It was a privilege to have lived."

NOTES

INTRODUCTION

1. Arthur Schopenhauer, "On Death and Its Relationship to the Indestructibility of Our Inner Nature," in Wolfgang Schirmacher, ed., *Philosophical Writings* (London: Continuum, 1994), p. 287.

1. SURELY THERE MUST BE SOME MISTAKE

1. Jill Bolte Taylor, *My Stroke of Insight* (New York: Viking, 2008).

2. LET YOUR ANGST BE YOUR UMBRELLA

1. Gestalt psychology, an early-twentieth-century holistic approach to human consciousness, maintains that our minds make sense of sensory information by distinguishing the significant data from the background. Like, "Hey, that's a wig in a bowl of spaghetti! Not a bunch of random squiggles!"

. . . .

4. Heideggerty-Dog, Ziggity-Boom, What You Do to Me

1. Martin Heidegger, *On Time and Being* (Chicago: University of Chicago Press, 2002), p. 6.

2. Ibid.

3. Quoted in Frank Kermode, *An Appetite for Poetry: Essays in Literary Interpretation* (Cambridge, MA: Harvard University Press, 1989), prologue.

4. Martin Heidegger, *Contributions to Philosophy (From Enowning)* (Bloomington: Indiana University Press, 1999).

5. T. Z. Lavine, *From Socrates to Sartre: The Philosophic Quest* (New York: Bantam, 1985), p. 332.

6. Jean-Paul Sartre, *Being and Nothingness*, in Stephen Priest, ed., *Basic Writings* (London: Routledge, 2001), p. 167.

6. The Eternal Now

1. Ludwig Wittgenstein, *Tractatus Logico-Philosophicus* (London: Routledge, 2001), § 6.4311.

2. According to the fifth-century B.C. Greek philosopher Zeno of Elea, if Achilles gives the tortoise a head start in the race, he will never be able to catch up with the tortoise. The reason for this is that Achilles first has to reach the point at which the tortoise started out, but by that time the tortoise has moved a bit. No matter how many times Achilles gets to the point where the tortoise last was—even if he does so an infinite number of times—he can never quite catch the tortoise.

7. Plato, the Godfather of Soul

1. Jerome H. Neyrey, "Soul," in *Harper's Bible Dictionary* (San Francisco: Harper & Row, 1985), pp. 982–3.

2. Matthew 16:26; Mark 8:36.

3. Neyrey, Ibid.

4. Ludwig Wittgenstein, *Philosophical Investigations*, 3rd ed. (Saddle River, NJ: Prentice Hall, 1973), § 622.

5. Plato, "Meno," *The Dialogues of Plato*, vol. 1, Benjamin Jowett, trans. (New York: Random House, 1937), pp. 349ff.

8. HEAVEN—A LANDSCAPE TO DIE FOR

1. A similar survey in Western European countries showed 49.4 percent of those surveyed said they believe in "life after death," while 19.2 percent said they believe in reincarnation. The survey results were reported by Erlendur Haraldsson, University of Iceland, in *Network*, no. 87, Spring 2005.

2. Adela Y. Collins, "Heaven," in *Harper's Bible Dictionary*, p. 377.

3. "Beulah Land" was a popular gospel hymn about Heaven, written by Edgar Page Stites in 1876. He later wrote, "I could write only two verses and the chorus, when I was overcome and fell on my face." Tori Amos wrote a song called "Beulah Land" for her 1998 album, *From the Choirgirl Hotel*.

4. Richard H. Hiers, "Kingdom of God," in *Harper's Bible Dictionary*, p. 528.

5. Adela Y. Collins, "Hades," in *Harper's Bible Dictionary*, p. 365.

6. 1 Thess. 4:16–17.

7. Micah 6:8

8. Luke 10:25.

9. Koran, 56:15ff.

10. Sunan al-Tirmidhi Hadith 2562.

9. TUNNEL VISION

1. William James, *The Varieties of Religious Experience* (New York: Modern Library, 1902), p. 378.

10. THE ORIGINAL KNOCK-KNOCK JOKE

1. These stories of the séance investigations of James, Sidgwick, and Munsterberg are found in Deborah Blum, *Ghost Hunters: William James and the Search for Scientific Proof of Life After Death* (New York: Penguin, 2006).

11. BEATING DEATH TO THE PUNCH LINE

1. Albert Camus, *The Myth of Sisyphus* (London: Vintage, 1991), p. 3.

2. Cicero, *De finibus bonorum et malorum*, H. Rackham, trans. (New York: Macmillan, 1924).

3. Seneca, "Epistulae morales," 70th epistle, in *Letters from a Stoic*, Robin Campbell, trans. (New York: Penguin Classics, 1969).

4. SciForums.com.

5. David Hume, "On Suicide," in *Essays on Suicide and the Immortality of the Soul* (Whitefish, MT: Kessinger, 2004), p. 8.

12. IMMORTALITY THROUGH NOT DYING

1. Michael Kinsley, "Mine Is Longer than Yours," *New Yorker*, April 7, 2008.

2. Manfred Clynes, "Time Consciousness in a Very Long Life," in *The Scientific Conquest of Death* (Buenos Aires: Libros en Red, 2004).

3. Lewis Thomas, "On Cloning a Human Being," *The Medusa and the Snail: More Notes of a Biology Watcher* (New York: Penguin, 1995), p. 52.

4. Michael Treder, "Upsetting the Natural Order," in ibid.

SUGGESTIONS FOR FURTHER READING

Aristotle. *De Anima*. London: Penguin, 1987.

Ballou, Robert, ed. *The Portable World Bible* (excerpts from scriptures of the world's religions). London: Penguin, 1977.

Blum, Deborah. *Ghost Hunters: William James and the Search for Scientific Proof of Life After Death*. New York: Penguin, 2006.

Becker, Ernest. *The Denial of Death*. New York: Free Press, 1973.

Camus, Albert. *The Myth of Sisyphus*. London: Penguin, 2000.

————. *The Stranger*. New York: Vintage, 1989.

Cicero. *De finibus bonorum et malorum*. New York: Macmillan, 1924.

Conrad, Mark, and Aeon Skoble, eds. *Woody Allen and Philosophy: You Mean My Whole Fallacy Is Wrong?* Chicago: Open Court, 2004.

Descartes, René. *Discourse on Method*. London: Penguin, 2000.

Freud, Sigmund. *Beyond the Pleasure Principle*. London: Penguin, 2003.

————. "The Future of an Illusion," in *Civilization, Society, and Religions*. London: Penguin, 1991.

Heidegger, Martin. *Being and Time*. San Francisco: Harper, 1962.

Husserl, Edmund. *The Essential Husserl*. Bloomington: Indiana University Press, 1999.

Immortality Institute. *The Scientific Conquest of Death*. Buenos Aires: Libros en Red, 2004.

James, William. "The Varieties of Religious Experience" and "Pragmatism," in *William James: Writings, 1902–1910*. New York: Library of America, 1988.

———. "The Will to Believe," in *William James: Writings, 1878–1899*. New York: Library of America, 1992.

Jung, C. G. "The Soul and Death," in Herman Feifel, ed., *The Meaning of Death*. New York: McGraw-Hill, 1959.

Kierkegaard, Søren. *The Concept of Anxiety*. Princeton, NJ: Princeton University Press, 1981.

———. *The Sickness unto Death*. London: Penguin, 1989.

Moody, Raymond. *Life After Life*. San Francisco: HarperOne, 2001.

Nietzsche, Friedrich. *The Gay Science*. New York: Vintage, 1974.

Plato. "Meno," in *Protagoras and Meno*. London: Penguin, 2006.

———. "Phaedo," in *The Last Days of Socrates*. London: Penguin, 2006.

———. *The Republic*. London: Penguin, 2007.

Rank, Otto. *Beyond Psychology*. Mineola, NY: Dover, 1958.

Ryle, Gilbert. *The Concept of Mind*. London: Penguin, 2000.

Sartre, Jean-Paul. *Being and Nothingness*. London: Routledge, 2003.

Schopenhauer, Arthur. *The World as Will and Idea*. Whitefish, MT: Kessinger, 2007.

Seneca. Epistulae morales, 70th epistle, in Robin Campbell, trans., *Letters from a Stoic*. New York: Penguin Classics, 1969.

Taylor, Jill Bolte. *My Stroke of Insight*. New York: Viking, 2008.

Tillich, Paul. "The Eternal Now," in *The Eternal Now*. New York: Scribner's, 1963.

Wrathall, Mark. *How to Read Heidegger*. New York: Norton, 2005.

Zimmer, Heinrich. *Philosophies of India*. Princeton, NJ: Princeton University Press, 1989.

INDEX